Children's ATLAS of God's

WORLD

Craig Froman

Master Books®
A Division of New Leaf Publishing Group

MY FATHER'S WORLD®

INTRODUCTION

First printing: June 2013

Master Books®, P.O. Box 726, Green Forest, AR 72638

Master Books® is a division of the New Leaf Publishing Group, Inc.

ISBN: 978-0-89051-706-2
Library of Congress Number: 2013904693

Cover by Diana Bogardus
Interior Design by
Diana Bogardus & Jennifer Bauer

Unless otherwise noted, Scripture quotations are from the New King James Version of the Bible.

Please consider requesting that a copy of this volume be purchased by your local library system.

Printed in China

Please visit our website for other great titles:

www.masterbooks.net

For information regarding author interviews, please contact the publicity department at (870) 438-5288

This book is dedicated to my precious family for their prayerful love and support.

Master Books®
A Division of New Leaf Publishing Group
www.masterbooks.net

There are many natural wonders in God's world . . . deserts, rainforests, frozen tundra, mountains, valleys, oceans, and more, including all the diversity of life. It is amazing when we realize just how much life fills our earth — a relatively small planet floating in space 93 million miles from the sun. Just as Job said, "He stretches out the north over empty space; He hangs the earth on nothing" (Job 26:7).

We really are flying as we float through space, as the Bible made clear, and fast! Did you know that the earth rotates about 1,000 miles per hour at the equator? Also, it revolves around the sun at about 66,600 miles per hour. And finally, it is traveling around the galaxy at about 500,000 miles per hour. Amazing!

JUST FOLLOW THE LINES! Though the earth is round, or at least somewhat pear shaped, it is shown flat on a map. Maps often include lines to mark distance for people who travel by plane or boat. Latitude is a created measure that marks how far north or south something is on the earth. These are shown on a map as horizontal lines, sometimes called parallels.

Longitude measurements are similar. They mark how far east or west something is on the earth, and are called meridians. These are shown on the map running from pole to pole. The Royal Observatory, Greenwich, in London, is on the prime meridian. This is the very first longitude line on a map or globe!

The directions on a compass are generally shown the same way on every map. You move north as you move up a map. You move south as you move down a map. You move east as you move right on a map. You move west as you move left on a map.

WHERE AND WHY TIME CHANGES! Most maps show both the land and the water on the earth. This includes rivers, lakes, and oceans, as well as mountains, deserts, forests, and more. Sometimes maps will show roadways, cities, and countries. Often they will show where certain time zones start and finish. Because the earth is so big, there are time zones to separate the hours. You see, it might be noon where you are, but midnight somewhere else! The 24 standard times zones around the world were developed in 1884 in an effort to coordinate time schedules for the railroad system.

WATER MAKES OUR PLANET BLUE! Though the largest areas of water on earth all cycle together, there are five distinct oceans recognized in the world. Here they are in order of size: the Pacific Ocean, Atlantic Ocean, Indian Ocean, Southern Ocean, and Arctic Ocean. The Pacific Ocean is the largest on earth, and is surrounded by an area of volcanic activity named "the Ring of Fire."

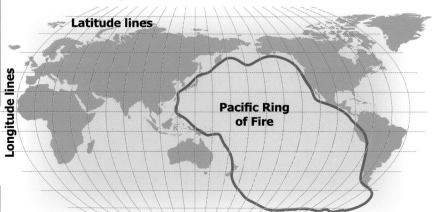

Latitude lines

Longitude lines

Pacific Ring of Fire

The deepest place in the ocean, the Challenger Deep in the Mariana Trench, lies deep below the Pacific. The longest underwater mountain range, the Mid-Atlantic

Ridge, is found in the Atlantic Ocean. In the southern region, tropical storms can turn into deadly hurricanes, while in the northern waters icebergs have been known to sink ships, the most famous being the 1912 RMS *Titanic* disaster.

The Indian Ocean borders eastern Africa, up to India, and across to Australia, and connects to the Red Sea, Arabian Sea, Persian Gulf, and Bay of Bengal. Much of the world's oil supply travels by ship across these waters. The most recently recognized ocean is the Southern Ocean around Antarctica and the southern hemisphere. On the northernmost part of earth and bordered by Europe, North America, and Asia is the Arctic Ocean, the smallest ocean and often covered in thick layers of ice.

GOD'S WONDERFUL PLAN! There are now over 7 billion people living on earth. We live in cities, called urban areas, as well as the country, or rural areas. It is estimated that 100 million people in the world are homeless. Some of this is because of war, or lack of jobs, or disasters that destroy homes. Remember to be thankful for your home and to pray about what you can do to help those in need. God put us all here to know Him and to show His love to others.

"In the beginning God created the heavens and the earth" (Genesis 1:1). This powerful verse written by Moses begins God's Word . . . the Bible. Here in Genesis we come to know that God made everything, including us, and that we can know that the world is no mere accident or caused by a random explosion in the universe. Our world was planned by Him, and we're a part of His great plan. Because we are all descendants of Adam and Eve, on earth there is really only one race of people . . . the human race.

GOD AND OUR CREATED WORLD! In the New Testament, Paul shared something similar many years later when talking with people who did not yet know of God. Paul said, "God, who made the world and everything in it, since He is Lord of heaven and earth, does not dwell in temples made with hands. Nor is He worshiped with men's hands, as though He needed anything, since He gives to all life, breath, and all things. And He has made from one blood every nation of men to dwell on all the face of the earth, and has determined their pre-appointed times and the boundaries of their dwellings, so that they should seek the Lord, in the hope that they might grope for Him and find Him, though He is not far from each one of us" (Acts 17:24–27). He mentioned again how the world was created by God, and how God brought all things to life on earth . . . and how every nation has come from His design. God desires everyone to know Him and His love.

This atlas is about God's amazing world. He has made it so diverse and fascinating, and we're still learning about it. It makes every day a wonder to wake up to. So let's start exploring!

"Indeed heaven and the highest heavens belong to the LORD your God, also the earth with all that is in it."

—Deuteronomy 10:14

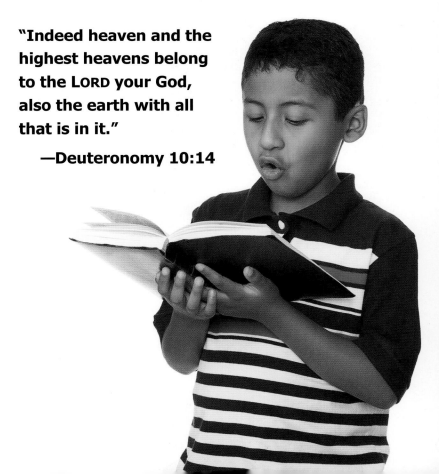

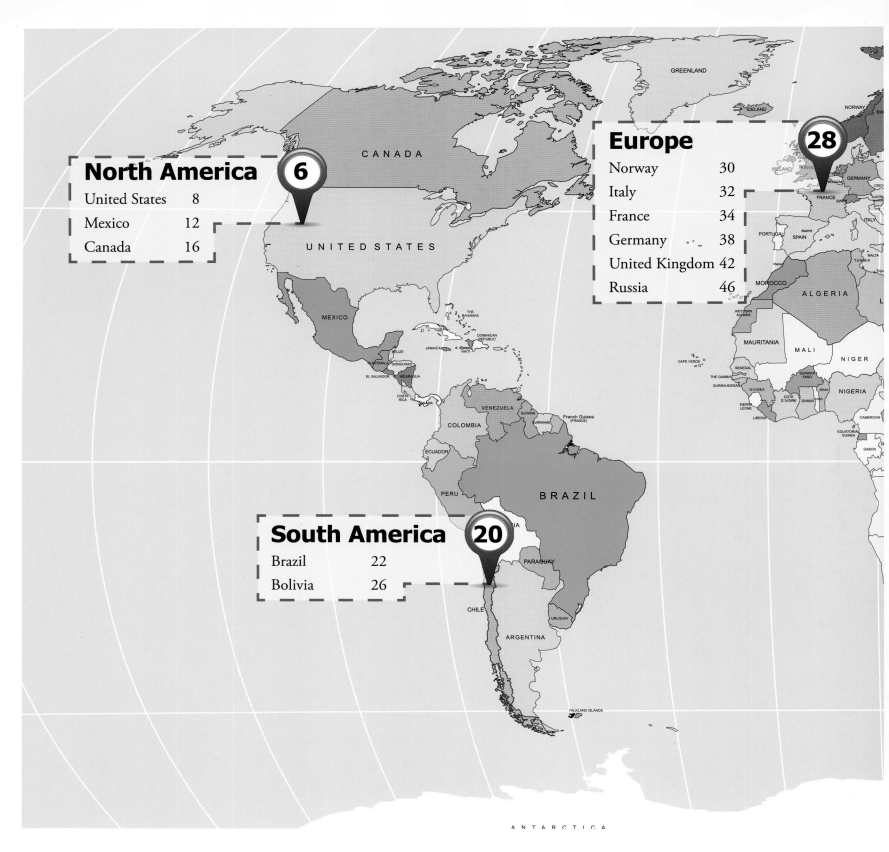

North America   6

United States	8
Mexico	12
Canada	16

Europe   28

Norway	30
Italy	32
France	34
Germany	38
United Kingdom	42
Russia	46

South America   20

Brazil	22
Bolivia	26

THE KEY TO YOUR CHILDREN'S ATLAS OF GOD'S WORLD

Welcome to your wondrous journey of God's amazing world! Here's what to watch for along the way to help you get the most out of each step.

Christian History & Tradition

The flag with the Cross marks information about Christian history, people of faith, and Christian traditions around the globe.

Red Pins

When you see a red pin in the book, you'll find that numbered pin on the map marking a landmark, a river, or other geographic location.

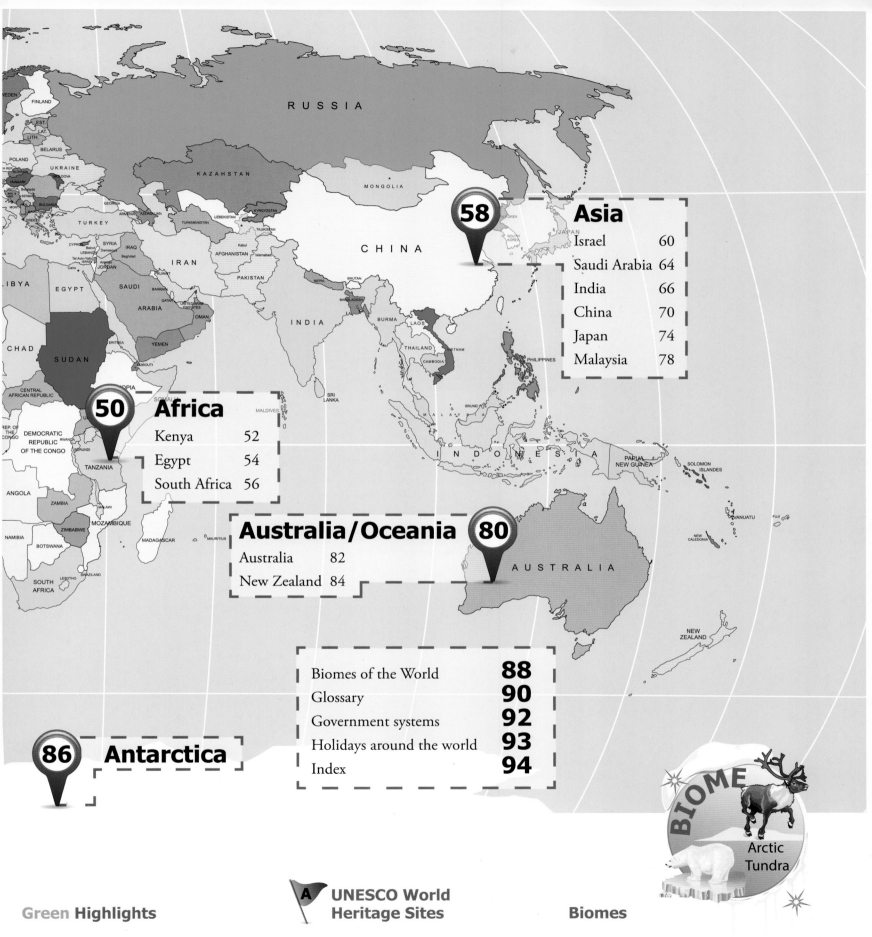

58

Asia

50

Africa

Australia/Oceania **80**

86 ## Antarctica

BIOME

Arctic
Tundra

Green Highlights

Words that are highlighted in green are cities or sites you'll find on the map, so peek over!

A UNESCO World Heritage Sites

The lettered green flags denote special sites recognized by the **U**nited **N**ations **E**ducational, **S**cientific, and **C**ultural **O**rganization. Look them all up at www.unesco.org

Biomes

Watch for the "Biomes" symbols to read about habitats around the world, including forests, deserts, grasslands, tundra, and more!

NORTH AMERICA

The continent of North America reaches from the coldest regions of **Canada** (the largest nation of North America at 3,855,103 square miles), down through the **United States** and **Mexico**, and all the way to the tropical islands of **Barbados, Trinidad, and Tobago**. Every biome of the earth can be found here. Biomes are communities of similar plants and animals. In North America they include the uplifted **Rocky Mountains** running down through Canada and the United States. You also find them in the tundra of the far north, wetlands of the south, deserts in the southwest, the grasslands of the great plains, deciduous forests of the east coast, rainforests of Central America, and islands in the Caribbean Sea.

① Begun in 1881, the work on the Panama Canal took over 30 years to finish. Since 1914, it has provided a waterway for ships passing through the narrow land area between the Gulf of Mexico and the Caribbean Sea. This 48-mile passage has locks at each end to raise ships up above sea level. A lock for ships is like a water elevator that can raise or lower them. The canal is considered by some to be one of the seven wonders of the modern world.

② Mount McKinley is the highest mountain on the continent of North America at 20,320 feet (6,194 meters). The first successful ascent was in 1913. It is also known as *Denali* (meaning "the high one" in the Athabaskan language of Koyukon), and typically takes three weeks to summit.

③ The largest island in the world is Greenland. It is geographically considered a part of North America, though Denmark in Europe still has some basic control of their foreign affairs and financial policies.

▶ Leif the Lucky introduced the gospel message to Greenland and possibly Vinland (Newfoundland) in as early as A.D. 1000. Christianity was accepted by the parliament (Alþingi) of Iceland at this time; the first time Christianity came to North America.

Viking ships often had ornately carved dragon heads on the prow or front of their longships. This fierce dragon symbol that often struck fear in the hearts of their enemies was very likely patterned after the last of the dinosaurs that survived beyond the Ice Age.

Capital City	Washington, D.C.
Government System	Federal republic; strong democratic tradition
Primary Languages	English and Spanish
Population	313,847,465
Monetary Unit	The dollar
Area	6,106,013 sq. miles
National Symbol	Bald eagle (bald refers to the white color)
National Anthem	"The Star-Spangled Banner"
Largest City	New York City 8,244,910

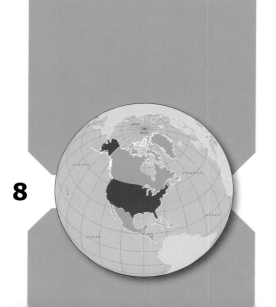

The United States is made up of 50 states, with two of these, **Alaska** and **Hawaii**, being separated from the other 48 by land or water. The United States has become the homeland for people from nearly every nationality, gaining it the name "the melting pot." The land stretches from Maine in the farthest northeast corner across to the islands of Hawaii far west in the Pacific Ocean and the **Aleutian Islands** of Alaska that are actually directly south of Russia.

1 Formally called the District of Columbia, Washington, D.C., is the capital city of the United States. Named after George Washington, the first president, this area was created for use by the federal government on July 16, 1790. It is not actually a part of any state. The United States Congress has authority over the mayor and the council of the District of Columbia.

2 Sculpted in the stone of the Black Hills of South Dakota and completed in 1941, Mount Rushmore National Memorial was designed and carved by Gutzon Borglum and his son, Lincoln Borglum. The four sculptures represent the likenesses of four U.S. presidents: George Washington, Thomas Jefferson, Theodore Roosevelt, and Abraham Lincoln, each about 60 feet high.

3 Once the longest suspension bridge in the world, the Golden Gate Bridge in San Francisco Bay is perhaps the most photographed bridge by far. A suspension bridge is one that has several tower structures with cables connecting them and giving the roadway support. Completed in 1937, it took four years to build.

American astronaut Neil Armstrong made history on July 20, 1969, as the first man to walk on the moon. The American flag still stands 238,712 miles away! Fellow astronaut and Christian Buzz Aldrin took part in a religious ceremony not broadcast to earth, as NASA had been sued for allowing Apollo 8 astronauts to read from the Bible.

Missionaries are associated with exotic lands — yet here you find amazing examples of those who devoted their lives to missions. From early European settlements to active ministry today, Christians like David Brainerd, who endured illness to share Christ with the Delaware Indian community, inspire others to serve.

On July 4, 1776, representatives from the then 13 colonies signed the Declaration of Independence. These signers appealed to God: "We hold these truths to be self-evident, that all men are created equal, that they are endowed by their Creator with certain unalienable Rights, that among these are Life, Liberty and the pursuit of Happiness."

CANADA

Seattle

Great Lakes

E

③ ⑤ A

Chicago

② ④ New York City

San Francisco

C Colorado River Denver

Missouri River

Washington DC ① Philadelphia

St. Louis

⑥

Los Angeles

Mississippi River

Atlanta

Dallas

MEXICO

D Miami

Gulf of Mexico

Lowlands/Hills/Mountains

CUBA

A
B
C
D

④ The Statue of Liberty was a gift to the United States from France. Frédéric Bartholdi designed the statue, which is an image of Libertas, a Roman goddess who represented freedom. The dedication took place on October 28, 1886, and has been a sign of freedom for millions who have entered the country. It stands on Liberty Island in New York Harbor and in her hands she holds a torch and a tablet that has the date July 4, 1776.

Arctic Ocean

RUSSIA

Alaska

Fairbanks

CANADA

Bering Sea

Anchorage

Juneau

Kodiak

Aleutian Islands   **Gulf of Alaska**

E
F

A. Yosemite National Park

B. Hawaii Volcanoes National Park

C. Mesa Verde National Park

D. Everglades National Park

E. Redwood National and State Parks

World Heritage Sites

Hawaii was the last of the 50 states, joining the Union in 1959. It is a grouping of volcanic islands located in the Pacific Ocean. The name *Hawaii* means "homeland," and comes from the Hawaiian language spoken on the islands.

Pacific Ocean

Honolulu

B

Hawaii

G
H

UNITED STATES

← **Navajo Indian boy in Native American traditional dress**

The Bald Eagle appears on the national Seal of the United States and is designated as the national bird. It faced localized extinction in the continental United States in the late 20th century. Populations have recovered so the species was removed from the U.S. government's list of endangered species in 1995 and transferred to the list of threatened species.

← **Bald Eagle**

George Washington, the first president, was known by those closest to him as a strong man of faith. In a book first published in 1842 called *Life of Washington* by Anna C. Reed, many who knew Washington gave firsthand accounts of his prayerful life. On one occasion, someone asked Mr. Secretary Thomson how he might recognize Mr. Washington from the others in Congress. Mr. Thomson replied, "You can easily distinguish him when Congress goes to prayers — Mr. Washington is the gentleman who kneels down."

Millions of bison used to roam the vast American grasslands. Often called buffalo, these massive mammals provided food, clothing, and even tools for Native Americans who hunted them. The ground would actually shake when the huge herds were running past. Sport hunting in the 1800s by non-Native Americans brought bison numbers to near extinction.

Thanksgiving in the United States is a special time for families to give thanks to the Lord for His many blessings. Always the fourth Thursday of November, the holiday is linked to the Pilgrims in 1621 who celebrated with the Wampanoag, a Native American people who helped them know the land and its best crops. The turkey is associated with the holiday, and was suggested for designation as the national bird by Benjamin Franklin.

In some marshes or bogs where there is less nitrogen for nutrients, some plants have been designed to find what they need by eating insects. These amazing plants include the Venus flytrap (shown above), found in certain areas of North and South Carolina.

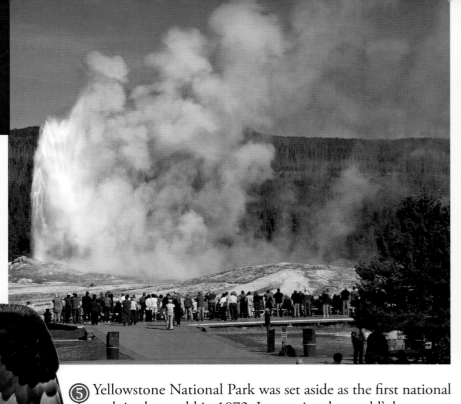

⑤ Yellowstone National Park was set aside as the first national park in the world in 1872. It contains the world's largest collection of geysers, and is within the states of Wyoming, Montana, and Idaho. Much of the landscape here is covered with trees. That forest land is mostly coniferous, which means having trees with cones and needles. Other kinds of forests include rainforests (forests with lots of rain and trees that never lose their leaves) and deciduous forests (forests with trees that lose their leaves in the fall).

⑥ The Grand Canyon, stretching 277 miles across Arizona, can be up to 18 miles wide and over a mile deep in places. The massive canyon was carved by the retreating waters after the Great Flood, revealing its deposits of sediment in the walls. The massive volcanic eruption of Mount St. Helens in 1980 showed the world the earth-transforming power a cataclysmic force can unleash in a very short amount of time, leaving behind canyons and other newly formed landscapes.

The Great Lakes can be seen clearly from outer space. NASA image. ➡

Great Lakes

Missouri River Basin

Mississippi River Basin

The Missouri River is the longest river in the United States at 2,341 miles in length. **The Mississippi River** is considered the largest river because of the amount of water it carries, starting in Lake Itasca, Minnesota, and flowing down to the Gulf of Mexico. **The Great Lakes** in the northeastern portion of North America consist of Lake Superior, Lake Michigan, Lake Huron, Lake Erie, and Lake Ontario, and contain just over 20 percent of the world's fresh water.

⬆ The point where the Missouri and Mississippi Rivers meet is found just north of St. Louis.

FLAG AND MEANING: There are three equal bands of green, white, and red; Mexico's coat of arms (an eagle with a snake in its beak perched on a cactus) is centered in the white band; green signifies hope, joy, and love; white represents peace and honesty; red stands for hardiness, bravery, strength, and valor. The coat of arms is derived from a legend that the wandering Aztec people were to settle at a location where they would see an eagle on a cactus eating a snake; the city they founded, Tenochtitlan, is now Mexico City.

Capital City	Mexico City
Government System	Federal republic
Primary Languages	Spanish
Population	114,975,406
Monetary Unit	Mexican peso
Area	1,220,606 sq. miles
National Symbol	Golden eagle
National Anthem	"Himno Nacional Mexicano" ("National Anthem of Mexico")
Largest City	Mexico City 8,851,080

The name *Mexico* is connected to the history of the people who lived here prior to the Spanish influence. It is a term related to the heart and people of the Aztec Empire. *Mexi* refers to a "beard of feathers" and the suffix *co* refers to the "place of the serpent," both of which are hints to the symbol on the Mexican flag. Because of the people who came from Spain to settle the area, there are actually more Spanish-speaking people here than there are in Spain! They mingled with the indigenous or native people who were living in the region. Bordering the southwest United States, the Hispanic cultural influence is strongest in those states. Border areas include **Baja California**, which is actually part of Mexico, not California as the name suggests. San Ysidro is the busiest border crossing between the two countries.

The breaking of a piñata is a wonderful way to celebrate a birthday or holiday. These colorful objects are often in the shape of animals, filled with candy or toys, and often made of papier-mâché. Although thought of as a Mexican tradition, it came originally from China, through Spain, and then to Mexico where they celebrate still by breaking them open to get to the prizes inside.

The axolotl or "water monster" is a rather odd-looking salamander. Most salamanders go through a change or metamorphosis to become more of a lizard-like creature. Axolotl adults actually keep their gills and live in the water all their lives. These creatures like to eat insects, worms, and small fish.

Diego Carranza was sent as a priest to Nejapa in Oaxaca, Mexico, in the late 1500s. There he served the Chontal Indians for 12 years to tell them of Jesus, and building places for them to worship. He helped construct a church in the village of Santa Maria Tequiztlan just before he died quite young because of complications of leprosy.

The Cathedral of Our Lady of Guadalupe is located in the city of Zamora. Construction began in 1898, but was halted at the turn of the 20th century by the Mexican Revolution. One can still see bullet holes in the cathedral wall from those who lost their lives for their faith.

The early Christians of the first century produced works of love that touched all people, including hospitals, orphanages, and relief for the oppressed. This legacy of love still shines in Mexico. Thousands of children left homeless by the war on drugs find relief in the Christian orphanages across the country.

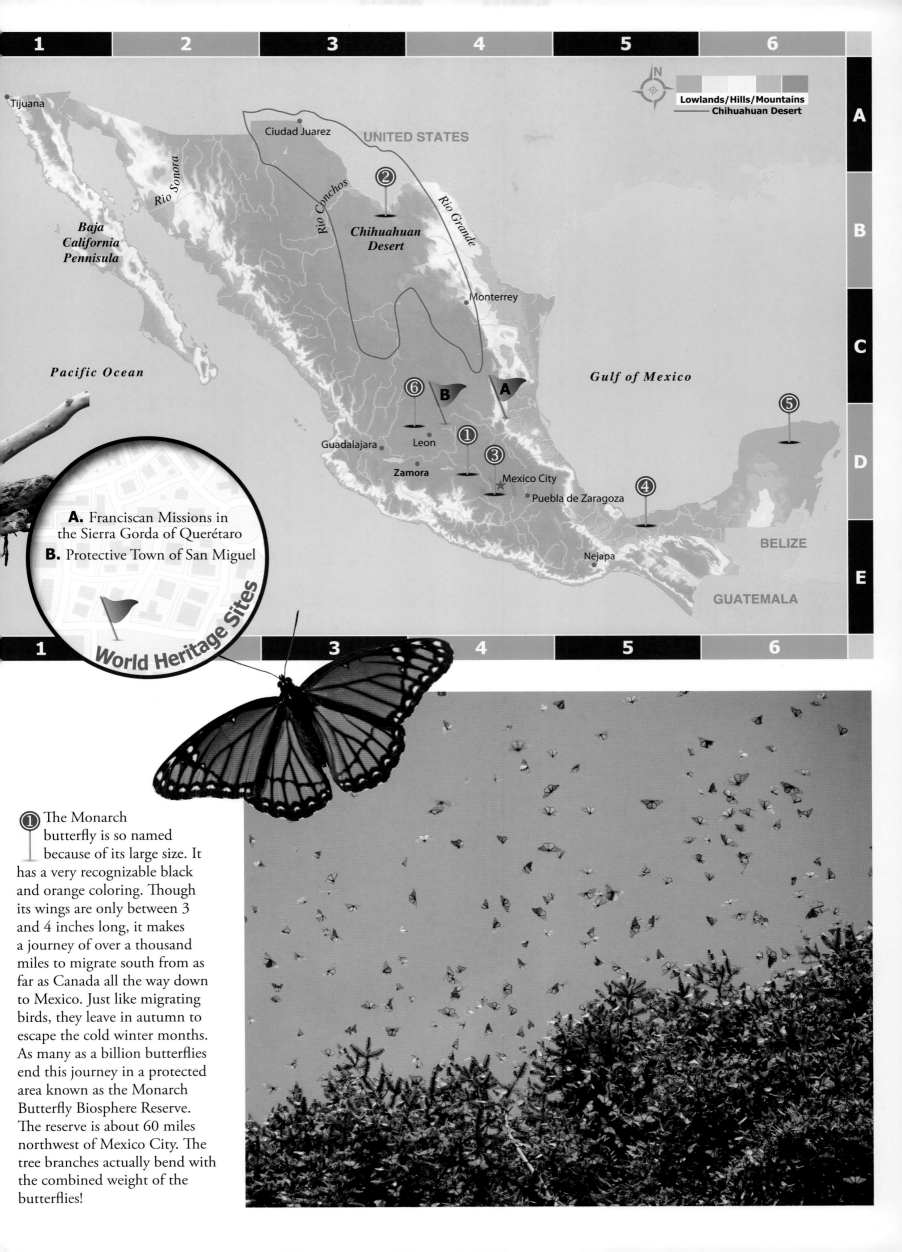

Tijuana

Ciudad Juarez

UNITED STATES

Rio Sonora

**Baja
California
Pennisula**

Rio Conchos

**Chihuahuan
Desert**

Rio Grande

Monterrey

Lowlands/Hills/Mountains
Chihuahuan Desert

A

B

C

Pacific Ocean

Gulf of Mexico

⑥

B

A

⑤

Guadalajara

Leon

①

③

Zamora

Mexico City

Puebla de Zaragoza

④

A. Franciscan Missions in
the Sierra Gorda of Querétaro
B. Protective Town of San Miguel

Nejapa

BELIZE

D

E

GUATEMALA

World Heritage Sites

① The Monarch butterfly is so named because of its large size. It has a very recognizable black and orange coloring. Though its wings are only between 3 and 4 inches long, it makes a journey of over a thousand miles to migrate south from as far as Canada all the way down to Mexico. Just like migrating birds, they leave in autumn to escape the cold winter months. As many as a billion butterflies end this journey in a protected area known as the Monarch Butterfly Biosphere Reserve. The reserve is about 60 miles northwest of Mexico City. The tree branches actually bend with the combined weight of the butterflies!

Many Mexican-style dishes are a mix of those the native people have eaten for hundreds of years along with the Spanish-style foods brought from Europe. There are foods made from beans and corn and peppers, as well as beef, chicken, and pork flavored with herbs and spices. Everything blends together into a very delicious, spicy cuisine known across the Americas and beyond.

"The ball game" seemed to be a quite popular sport among the Mayans and Toltecs of certain regions of Mexico. It involved two teams trying to toss a stone ball through carved stone rings. During certain religious festivals, the team that lost was often sacrificed!

In the center of Mexico, women dancers wear ruffled and tiered long skirts in white or bright colors, trimmed with colorful ribbons and lace. Often seen in traditional celebrations, the wide-brimmed hats which have become a cultural and national symbol of Mexico are called *sombreros*. They can be simple straw or more elaborately decorated felt.

Gila monsters thrive in dry, desert climates. These poisonous lizards actually move very slowly, and are covered with colored scales that look like beads.

② Deserts can be hot or cold, but they are most often dry places that receive less than 10 inches of rain each year. In colder desert climates, the water is frozen. In warmer areas, the few plants that grow are specially designed to hold in moisture. Certain grasses and cacti do well and provide shelter for various creatures. The Chihuahuan Desert of northern Mexico receives most of its rain during the late summer monsoon season. Early winter provides a small amount of additional rain. Including portions that reach into the southern United States, this is North America's second largest desert.

The saguaro is a type of cactus that can grow over 60 feet tall! While some live more than 150 years, it can take 75 years for just the side arm to fully develop. They were designed by God to grow fastest during the heaviest rains when growth is best sustained.

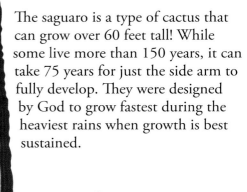

BIOME

Desert

③ The ruins of the Aztec city called Tenochtitlán are still seen from the present capital. Just north of Mexico City lies the remains of the religious center of this powerful people. Spanish soldiers led by Fernando Cortés were the first known Europeans to see the great city. It included a vast complex of pyramids and buildings aligned with the stars.

④ A thriving community some 1,300 years ago, Palenque was a Mayan city that disappeared into the jungle until it was rediscovered in the 1700s. The beautifully crafted buildings are covered with sculpted figures from Mayan myths. The history of this ancient place can now be retold as historians read through the ancient hieroglyphs.

⑤ Over a million people each year visit the great ruins at Chichen Itza. Nearly a thousand years ago this became the center of a great Mayan civilization in the Yucatán peninsula. The buildings that have endured time include the circular observatory known as El Caracol, and the Warrior's Temple. The name Chichen Itza means "at the mouth of the well of the Itza."

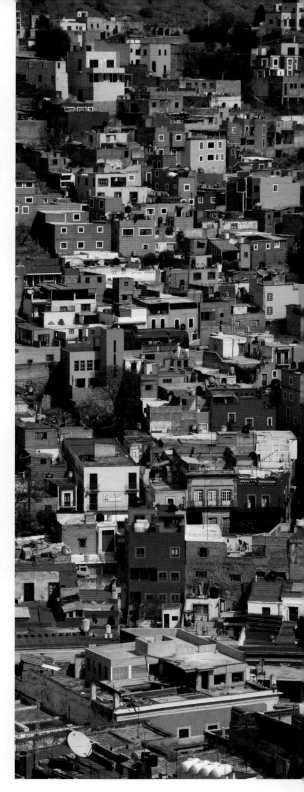

⑥ The historic town of Guanajuato was first settled in 1520 by the Spaniards. Its name means "Frog Hill." Soon after, they discovered rich deposits of silver. The town thrived for over 300 years and blessed the surrounding area with churches, hospitals, and even palaces. It is known for its Baroque-style buildings, as well as its subterranean streets.

The Day of the Dead is a national holiday in Mexico. Friends and family gather to remember and pray for loved ones who have died. Held on November 1 and 2, it is celebrated with the Catholic holidays of All Saint's Day and All Soul's Day, as well as echoing ancient ceremonies honoring an Aztec goddess who ruled over festivals of the dead. Little sugar candies shaped like skulls, marigolds, and favorite foods, and visits to the graves of loved ones are part of the activities.

FLAG AND MEANING:

There are two bands of red with a white square between them; an 11-pointed red maple leaf is centered in the white square. The maple leaf has long been a Canadian symbol, and the official colors of Canada are red and white.

Capital City	Ottawa
Government System	Parliamentary democracy, federation, and constitutional monarchy
Primary Languages	English and French
Population	34,300,083
Monetary Unit	Canadian dollar
Area	6,204,186 sq. miles
National Symbol	Maple leaf
National Anthem	"O Canada"
Largest City	Toronto 5,583,064

Canada is the largest nation by land area in North America. It is made of up of the ten provinces of Alberta, British Columbia, Manitoba, New Brunswick, Newfoundland and Labrador, Nova Scotia, Ontario, Prince Edward Island, Quebec, and Saskatchewan. Canada also has three territories: the Northwest Territories, Nunavut, and Yukon. Settled by both English- and French-speaking people, the province of Québec is home to the majority of Canadians who speak French. These early French settlers were farmers and fur traders. **Montreal** is actually the second-largest French-speaking city in the world, next to Paris. The majority of Canadians live within 100 miles of their border with the United States. Yonge Street, near **Toronto**, is over 1,100 miles long and has been called the longest street in the world.

The longest national highway in the world is the Trans-Canada Highway (T.C.H.). It runs approximately 4,860 miles on a path across southern Canada, from St. John's, Newfoundland, in the east to Victoria, British Columbia, in the west.

Polar bears are the largest of the land predators. They use their large paws to help them swim, sometimes going as far as 100 miles in a day. The rough surfaces on the bottom help them keep from slipping on the ice. Their fur and skin were created by God to soak up sunlight to keep them warm!

Canada's massive oil reserves are found in the oil sands reserves in Alberta. Venezuela and Saudi Arabia are the only two countries with more oil.

The sport of lacrosse has been played by native Canadians for over 900 years. The name means "the stick." It was first called this by Jesuit missionary, martyr, and historian Jean de Brébeuf, in 1637. Sometimes involving as many as a thousand men on the field, it would be played from sunrise to sunset.

Reginald Fessenden was born in Quebec, Canada, the eldest son of an Anglican minister. He did early work with radio, being the first to transmit his voice without wires, reading portions of Scripture. He also created inventions in sonar and television.

Canada has a rich Christian heritage. In 1960, the prime minister introduced the Canadian Bill of Rights. The opening declaration states: "The Parliament of Canada, affirming that the Canadian Nation is founded upon principles that acknowledge the supremacy of God…."

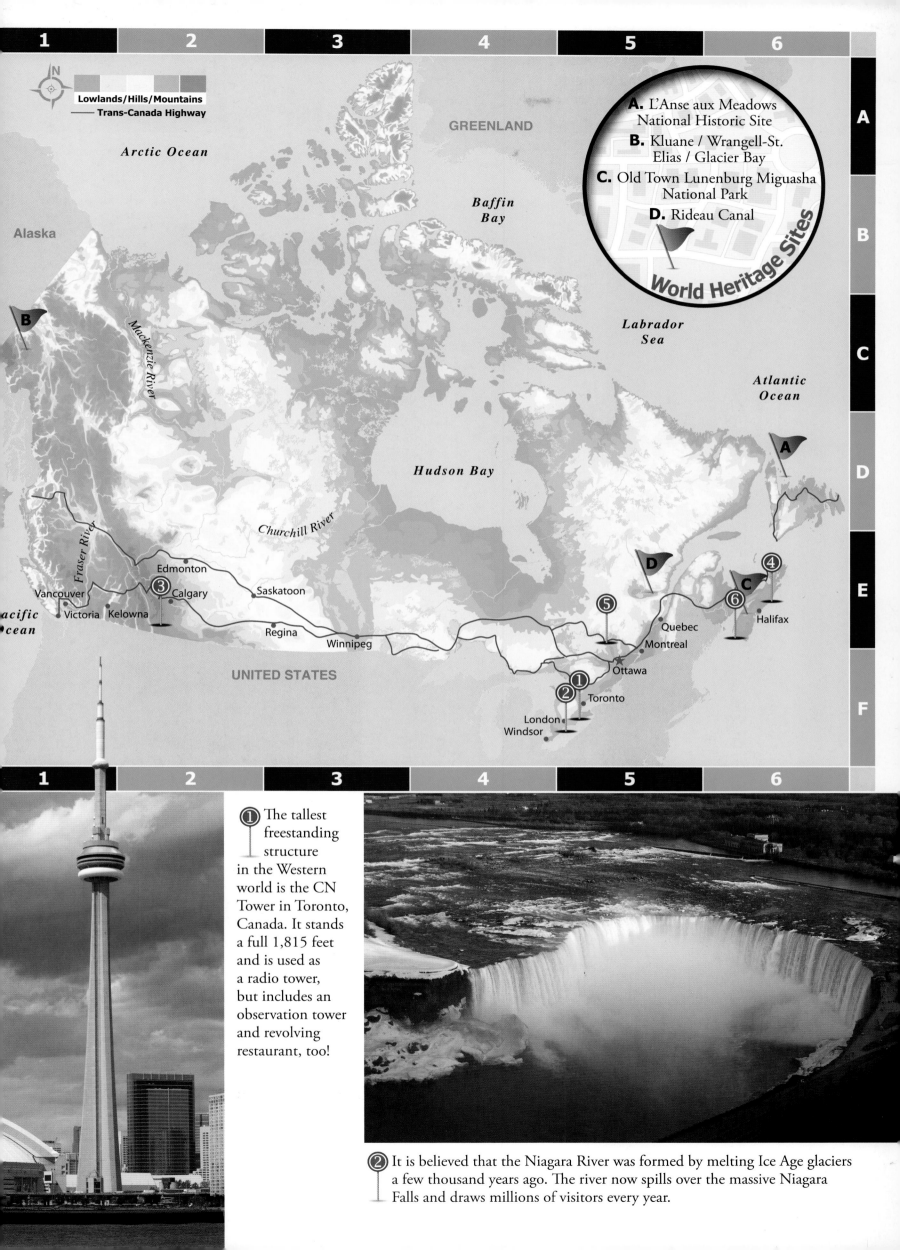

Lowlands/Hills/Mountains
— Trans-Canada Highway

GREENLAND

Arctic Ocean

Baffin Bay

Alaska

Mackenzie River

Labrador Sea

Atlantic Ocean

Hudson Bay

Churchill River

Fraser River

Edmonton
③ Calgary
Saskatoon
Vancouver
Victoria Kelowna
Regina
Winnipeg
⑤
Quebec
Montreal
⑥ C ④
Halifax
D

★ Ottawa
② ①
Toronto
London
Windsor

UNITED STATES

Pacific Ocean

World Heritage Sites

A. L'Anse aux Meadows National Historic Site
B. Kluane / Wrangell-St. Elias / Glacier Bay
C. Old Town Lunenburg Miguasha National Park
D. Rideau Canal

① The tallest freestanding structure in the Western world is the CN Tower in Toronto, Canada. It stands a full 1,815 feet and is used as a radio tower, but includes an observation tower and revolving restaurant, too!

② It is believed that the Niagara River was formed by melting Ice Age glaciers a few thousand years ago. The river now spills over the massive Niagara Falls and draws millions of visitors every year.

CANADA

Ice hockey is a very important sport for Canadians, helping provide entertainment and exercise during the cold, frozen winters. A sporting game that involved a curved stick and a ball has been discovered in images dating back thousands of years to Egypt. The first notion of the modern-style game of ice hockey appears in Ireland during the Middle Ages. It became popular in Canada in the mid to late 1800s.

Lacrosse

Basketball

Canadian physical education instructor Dr. James Naismith invented the game of basketball in 1891. He was teaching at Springfield College in Springfield, Massachusetts, at the time.

⬇ **Magnetic North Pole**

The magnetic north pole is located in northern Canada, though it moves continually, about 40 miles each year. A compass actually points north because of magnetic changes in the core of the earth, which is made of iron.

⬆ **Ice hockey**

The Inuit are a native people group of Canada, as well as the United States, Russia, and Greenland. They have lived in the coldest regions of the world, even inhabiting some of the northernmost places in the Canadian tundra. It is thought by many that the first Inuit people crossed a bridge of ice that once existed between what is now Alaska and Russia during the Ice Age after the Great Flood of Noah.

Arctic foxes roam some of the coldest climates in Canada. Though about the size of a house cat, they are a part of the dog family. In the summer their fur is anywhere from brown to grey in color. However, God designed their coats to change to a snow white in the winter to protect and hide them.

The Royal Canadian Mounted Police, better known as Mounties, guard the majority of the country as a special police force. Known best by their famous red uniforms, many also wear uniforms similar to police in other countries. They have been protecting the people of their nation since 1873.

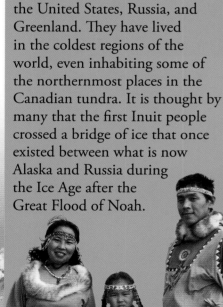

The five major agricultural industries in Canada are: (1) the growing of grains, (2) beef and hogs, (3) dairy, (4) poultry and eggs, and (5) horticulture. The nation is one of the largest exporters in the world. Among farm animals, the highest number is beef cattle, with numbers of over 12.7 million in recent years. Large farms throughout Canada help provide an abundance of the world's wheat crop. Also, Canadian forests cover more land area than any country other than Russia or Brazil.

③ Waterton Lakes National Park is filled with many kinds of rare or threatened plants, and everything from prairie to mountains.

④ Old Town Lunenburg was developed in a planned British settlement pattern that has stayed the same since 1753!

⑤ The parliament building of Canada overlooking Rideau Canal.

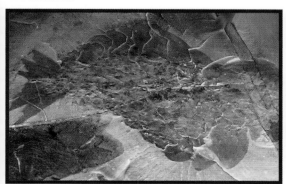

The Burgess Shale Formation within the Canadian Rockies in British Columbia has proven to be among the richest sources of dinosaur and other fossils in the world. Known for the amazing preservation of the specimens, it was discovered by paleontologist Charles Walcott in 1909.

← Centrosaurus

The Canadian provinces of Alberta and British Columbia have been sites of unique and wonderful fossil discoveries. Albertosaurus, Edmontosaurus, Lambeosaurus, and Edmontonia are named for their Canadian connections. Over 35 different dinosaurs, including Centrosaurus, have been discovered in Dinosaur Provincial Park, near the center of the badlands of Alberta.

⑥ World famous fossil cliffs on the Bay of Fundy, at Joggins, Nova Scotia. Canada has the longest coastal area of any nation in the world. The European explorer who opened up this vast region to the world was John Cabot in 1497. This Italian navigator was commissioned by Henry VII of England to find another route to the Spice Islands. He actually landed in Newfoundland.

SOUTH AMERICA

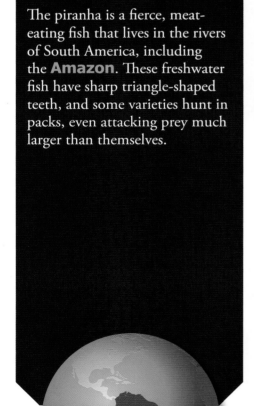

The piranha is a fierce, meat-eating fish that lives in the rivers of South America, including the **Amazon**. These freshwater fish have sharp triangle-shaped teeth, and some varieties hunt in packs, even attacking prey much larger than themselves.

The northernmost tip of South America dips into the warm waters of the Caribbean. It journeys across vast rainforests, steep mountain ranges, and down to the southernmost tip of **Cape Horn** near the frozen Antarctic. It is a land richly blended with the cultures of the original native peoples along with the influx of Spanish, Portuguese, African, and Asian customs. In 2013, Cardinal Jorge Mario Bergoglio of Argentina was selected as the new pope of the Catholic Church; the first ever from the Americas.

① Stretching over 4,300 miles, the Andes is the longest mountain range in the world, and many of the highest peaks are volcanoes. These include Ojos de Salado, which rises over 22,600 feet. Over 50 of the world's highest active volcanoes can be found in the Andes. They cross the countries of Argentina, Bolivia, Chile, Colombia, Ecuador, Peru, and Venezuela.

② Machu Picchu is an ancient city of the Inca and means "old mountain." It was rediscovered in 1911 by American Hiram Bingham while exploring in a remote area of the Andes Mountains of Peru. This is a monument to the skilled stone craftsmanship of the workers who carved blocks of granite to fit together with great accuracy and without the need for mortar.

③ On Easter Sunday in 1722, Dutch explorer Jacob Roggeveen landed on the remote island of Rapa Nui, naming it Easter Island to honor the sacred day of Christ's Resurrection. Though considered part of Chile since 1888, it is over 2,300 miles away, in the Pacific Ocean. Easter Island is best known for the massive stone sculptures called *moai*, some weighing 50 tons.

④ Aconcagua is the highest mountain on the continent of South America at 22,841 feet (6,961 meters). The first successful ascent was in 1897. Taking anywhere from two to three weeks to reach the summit, *Aconcagua* means either "comes from the other side" or "stone sentinel." The original meaning is lost because the name comes either from the Arauca, Quechua, or Aymara languages.

South America is the world's leader in beef exports, with Brazil leading all other countries. *Churrasco* is a Spanish term that refers to grilled beef or other meats, often served with garlic, peppers, and olive oil. It is very popular throughout many of the Latin American countries.

A
B
C
D
E
F
G

CARAGUA

COSTA RICA

PANAMA

Caracas ★

TRINIDAD AND TOBAGO

Atlantic Ocean

Orinoco

VENEZUELA

⑤

Georgetown ★

GUYANA

Paramaribo ★

SURINAME

Cayenne ★

FRENCH GUIANA

Bogota ★

COLOMBIA

Negro

Amazon

Amazon

Equator

Quito ★

ECUADOR

Amazon

Madeira

BRAZIL

ALAPAGOS ANDS

PERU

②

Lima ★

BOLIVIA

La Paz ★

Brasilia ★

Sucre ★

③ Tropic of Capricorn

ASTER LAND

①

PARAGUAY

Tropic of Capricorn

CHILE

Asuncion ★

Parana

④

Pacific Ocean

URUGUAY

Atlantic Ocean

Santiago ★

Buenos Aires ★

Montevideo ★

ARGENTINA

⑥

FALKLAND ISLANDS

Stanley ★

SOUTH GEORGIA ISLAND

Cape Horn

⑤ The highest uninterrupted waterfall in the world is Angel Falls in Venezuela, falling some 2,648 feet.

⑥ The Glacier Perito Moreno in the Los Glaciares National Park is located in the Austral Andes of Argentina. The ice field is considered to be the largest ice mantle on the planet with the exception of Antarctica. Most of the glacier activity here can be seen in and around Lake Argentino and Lake Viedma. The glaciers in the park are some of the few in the world actually growing.

BRAZIL

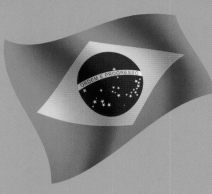

FLAG AND MEANING:
There is a green background with a large yellow diamond in the center bearing a blue celestial globe with 27 white, five-pointed stars. The globe has a white, equatorial band with the motto *ORDEM E PROGRESSO* (Order and Progress). The green represents the forests of the country, the yellow its mineral wealth, while the blue circle and stars depict the sky over Rio de Janeiro on the morning of November 15, 1889, the day the Republic of Brazil was declared.

Capital City	Brasilia
Government System	Federal republic
Primary Languages	Portuguese
Population	199,321,413
Monetary Unit	Brazilian real
Area	5,290,899 sq. miles
National Symbol	Southern Cross constellation
National Anthem	"Hino Nacional Brasileiro" ("Brazilian National Anthem")
Largest City	São Paulo 11,316,149

Brazil is actually the fifth-largest country in the world by area, with just over half of all people in South America living here. Though most countries in South America speak Spanish as a main language, Brazil was developed by many people from Portugal. For this reason, the official language is Portuguese. The country is named after the brazilwood tree. The tree can be used to create a red dye, which was popular in Europe hundreds of years ago. The **Amazon River** flows to the Atlantic Ocean and is the second longest river in the world.

Capybaras or capivaras are the world's largest rodents. Some call them "water pigs" because of their size and as they live around water, including rivers, marshes, lakes, swamps, and tropical forests. They most often feed on grasses.

Toucan ➡

⬆ Capybaras

About one-fourth of the world's coffee is produced in Brazil.

Toucans are some of the most recognizable birds in the world. Though it looks heavy, the multicolored beak is actually very light, made of bone with spongy tissue. They use them to reach fruit, which is their main food. These amazing beaks can also help them regulate their body temperatures!

The Yanomami people are native or indigenous people who live in the area between Venezuela and Brazil. There are between 200 and 250 Yanomami villages within the **Amazon rainforest**. The people of each village live in a *shabono*, a circular building with an open area in the middle.

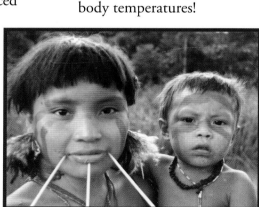

Christianity was introduced to Brazil as far back as the 1500s. When Portugal claimed the country as their own, the first official act was to call this land the "Island of the Holy Cross." The Roman Catholic Church became the dominant faith for the next 400 years.

Christ the Redeemer is the fifth-largest statue of Jesus in the world. It stands atop Corcovado Mountain overlooking the city of Rio de Janeiro, and is 99 feet tall. Constructed in the early part of the 20th century, it has become a profound symbol of Brazilian Christianity.

The Church in Brazil is growing at a fast pace, especially compared to many areas of the Western world where Christianity seems to be stagnant or in decline. This vital country of faith also has a thriving economy, and even after the global crisis they send out more missionaries than any country other than the United States.

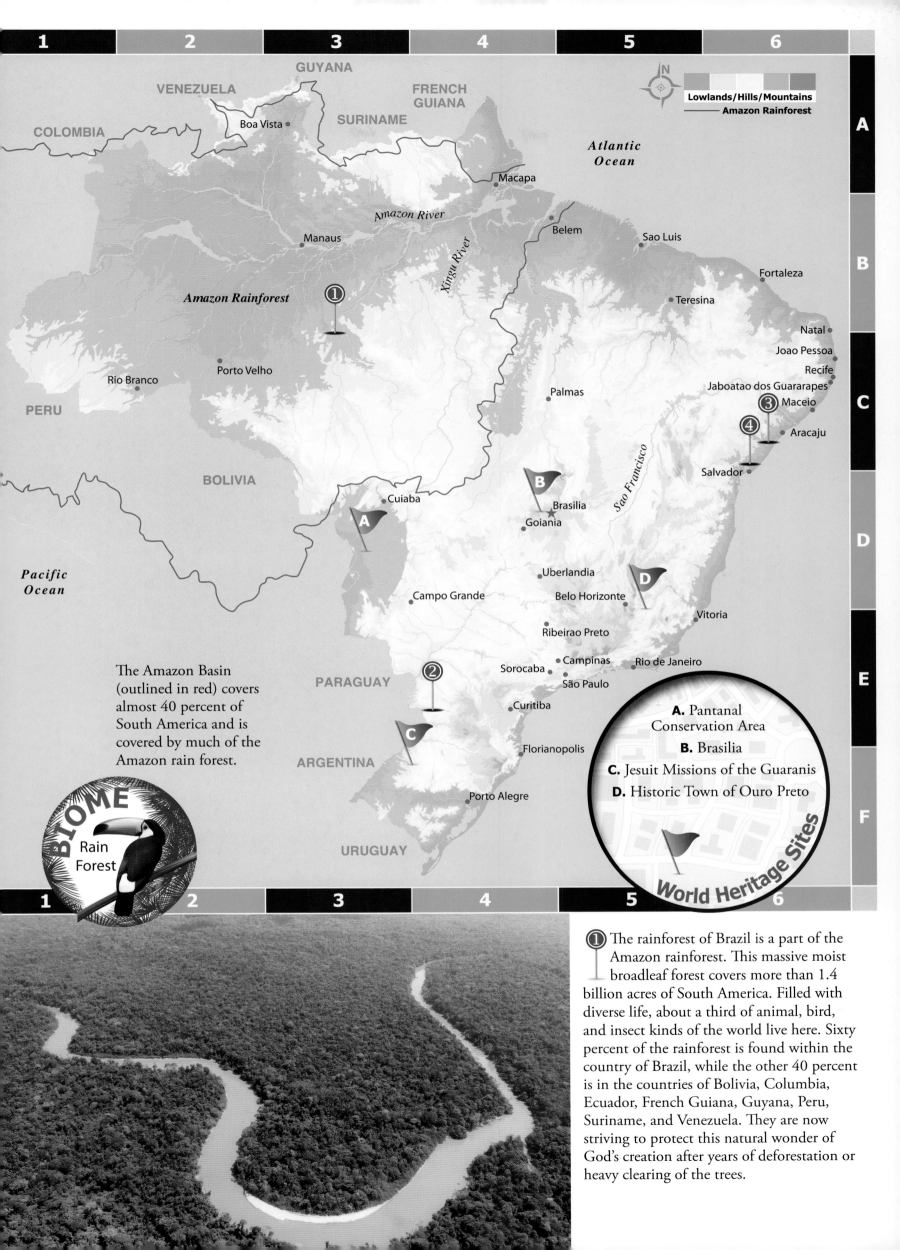

| | 1 | 2 | 3 | 4 | 5 | 6 |

COLOMBIA

VENEZUELA

GUYANA

Boa Vista

SURINAME

FRENCH GUIANA

Macapa

Atlantic Ocean

Amazon River

Manaus

Belem

Sao Luis

Xingu River

A

Amazon Rainforest

①

Fortaleza

Teresina

Natal

Joao Pessoa

Recife

Jaboatao dos Guararapes

③ Maceio

④

Aracaju

Salvador

Porto Velho

Rio Branco

Palmas

PERU

BOLIVIA

Sao Francisco

B Brasilia

★

Cuiaba

A

Goiania

Uberlandia

D

Campo Grande

Belo Horizonte

Vitoria

Ribeirao Preto

Pacific Ocean

The Amazon Basin (outlined in red) covers almost 40 percent of South America and is covered by much of the Amazon rain forest.

PARAGUAY

②

Sorocaba

Campinas

Rio de Janeiro

São Paulo

Curitiba

C

Florianopolis

ARGENTINA

URUGUAY

Porto Alegre

BIOME

Rain Forest

Lowlands/Hills/Mountains
— Amazon Rainforest

A. Pantanal Conservation Area

B. Brasilia

C. Jesuit Missions of the Guaranis

D. Historic Town of Ouro Preto

World Heritage Sites

| | 1 | 2 | 3 | 4 | 5 | 6 |

① The rainforest of Brazil is a part of the Amazon rainforest. This massive moist broadleaf forest covers more than 1.4 billion acres of South America. Filled with diverse life, about a third of animal, bird, and insect kinds of the world live here. Sixty percent of the rainforest is found within the country of Brazil, while the other 40 percent is in the countries of Bolivia, Columbia, Ecuador, French Guiana, Guyana, Peru, Suriname, and Venezuela. They are now striving to protect this natural wonder of God's creation after years of deforestation or heavy clearing of the trees.

Amazon Rainforest Layers

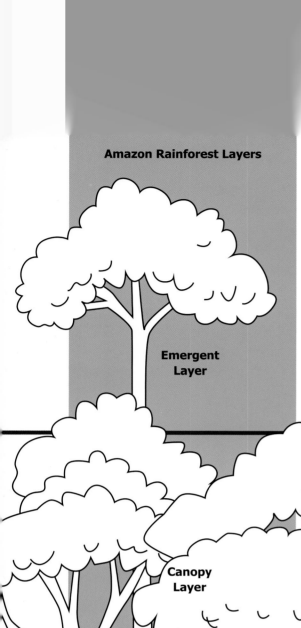

Emergent Layer

Canopy Layer

Understory Layer

Forest Floor

The Amazonian rainforest covers 1.4 billion acres, crossing the boundaries of nine different nations. The area is said to be named for the women who fought fiercely as part of their tribes in a war against Spanish adventurer Francisco de Orellana.

EMERGENT LAYER: This layer has the tallest trees in the rainforest, some growing over 200 feet tall with fairly small leaves and few branches. There are also small monkeys here, along with bats, birds, and insects.

One of the largest of rainforest birds is the Rhinoceros hornbill. They often live their entire lives in the tops of the trees, growing up to four feet long! God designed their beak to be lightweight, even though it's so large. They use it to build their nests, gather food, and make their distinctive calls.

CANOPY LAYER: The majority of animals in the rainforest live in this layer. Sunlight can reach the top portion but rarely down below. Frogs, insects, lizards, monkeys, and sloths fill the sunlit shadows here.

Woolly monkeys live throughout the forests of South America. They can actually use their tails like an additional hand or foot. This kind of tail is called a prehensile tail. Living in large family groups for safety, they thrive on fruits and seeds for their meals.

UNDERSTORY LAYER: This is a layer of high humidity and very little light. There are small trees and shrubs growing in the shade, along with birds, butterflies, and some snakes.

The Emperor tamarins may well have been named after Emperor Wilhelm II of Germany. Their facial hairs resemble a long, white mustache! These primates live in the trees for safety, sleeping there as well, but do sometimes run along the forest floor. In the trees they can find the fruit, flowers, and insects they love so much. Their calls are very loud, and are often used to warn off other tamarins entering their territory.

FOREST FLOOR LAYER: Little sunlight ever reaches the forest floor, so few plants hinder one from walking here. In the soil covered with wet leaves and twigs, one finds ants, earthworms, and termites. Larger animals include gorillas, jaguars, and leopards.

Leafcutter ants thrive in South America, cutting leaves and grass for their meals. They develop very complex underground nests that can stretch out more than 250 feet across, and have millions of ants working together within it.

② The Iguazu Falls in the Iguazu National Park is a vast and lush area on the border of Brazil and Argentina. The name *Iguazu* literally means "big water," and it truly is, at over 250 feet high in parts and almost two miles wide. The water from the falls passes down many cascades, creating a spray of mist that soaks the surrounding forest. The forest here is filled with wildlife, including anteaters, howler monkeys, jaguars, ocelots, and more.

③ In 1549 the first priests of the Society of Jesus came to Brazil to bring the message of Christ to the "new world." Franciscan monks arrived soon after in 1585. São Francisco Square, in the town of São Cristovão is an example of the heritage they left behind. The São Francisco Church and convent were finished in 1693, with much of the town being built in the 18th and 19th centuries.

④ The Historic Center of the Town of Olinda is filled with colorful buildings and colorful history as well. It dates back to the sugar cane produced here in the 16th century. Sugar cane is still considered one of the world's largest crops. In Olinda a legacy of faith is still seen within the 20 baroque-style churches, as well as the convents and chapels. The city also includes beautiful gardens and houses painted in vibrant colors or covered in tiles.

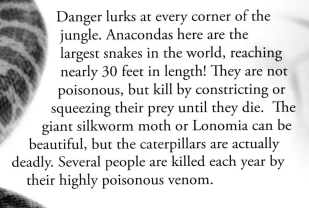

Danger lurks at every corner of the jungle. Anacondas here are the largest snakes in the world, reaching nearly 30 feet in length! They are not poisonous, but kill by constricting or squeezing their prey until they die. The giant silkworm moth or Lonomia can be beautiful, but the caterpillars are actually deadly. Several people are killed each year by their highly poisonous venom.

← **Anaconda**

Caterpillar of a giant silkworm moth →

BOLIVIA

FLAG AND MEANING: There are three horizontal bands of red, yellow, and green, with the coat of arms centered on the yellow band. The red stands for bravery and the blood of national heroes, yellow for the nation's mineral resources, and green for the fertility of the land.

Capital City	La Paz
Government System	Republic
Primary Languages	Spanish
Population	10,290,003
Monetary Unit	Boliviano
Area	682,626 sq. miles
National Symbol	Llama; Andean condor
National Anthem	"Cancion Patriotica" ("Patriotic Song")
Largest City	Santa Cruz 1,841,282

Maned wolves live mainly on the grasslands, and are sometimes called skunk wolves because of their bad odor. Their long legs help them see above the tall grassy blades, and the mane stands up when the animal feels danger.

The country of Bolivia is named after Simón Bolívar. It became an independent nation on August 6, 1825. From the lowlands in the east, to the great **Andes Mountains**, it holds much-varied landscapes. It is also completely encircled by five other countries, so it has no ocean shoreline. Bolivia has a great wealth of natural resources, including petroleum, tin, and other metals, lumber, fishing, mining, and more. Because the population here is so varied, from backgrounds that include native peoples, Europeans, Africans, and Asians, there is a great diversity in the arts, foods, and music as well.

The Uros people live upon constructed, floating islands made of bundled reeds on Lake Titicaca in Bolivia and Peru. The floating islands were a form of defense against aggressive nearby tribes. Houses built on the man-made islands could hold as few as two or three, or even as many as ten people.

Pumapunku is a mysterious site featuring block-like large stones with precise holes and edges. Known by its examples of skilled construction, it is located near the temple complex of Tiwanaku where the Incas believed the world was created.

The Christian message was first introduced as far back as 1552 in the town of La Plata. Many different religious groups came, including the Franciscans and Jesuits mostly from Europe. Now the majority of Bolivians consider themselves to be Christians, either Catholic or Protestant.

Christmas is one of the most important holidays for many Christians throughout Bolivia. Christmas Eve is a special time, called the *Misa del Gallo*, or mass of the rooster. At midnight, bells ring and the people celebrate, often not returning home until early morning, or the time of the rooster's crowing.

Reports indicate that nearly 60 percent of people in Bolivia live in huts that are constructed of adobe. The vinchuca bug lives in adobe and it can spread disease. The Habitat for Humanity in Bolivia is a Christian outreach effort established here in 1985. Habitat helps build brick and cement homes that are safer for residents.

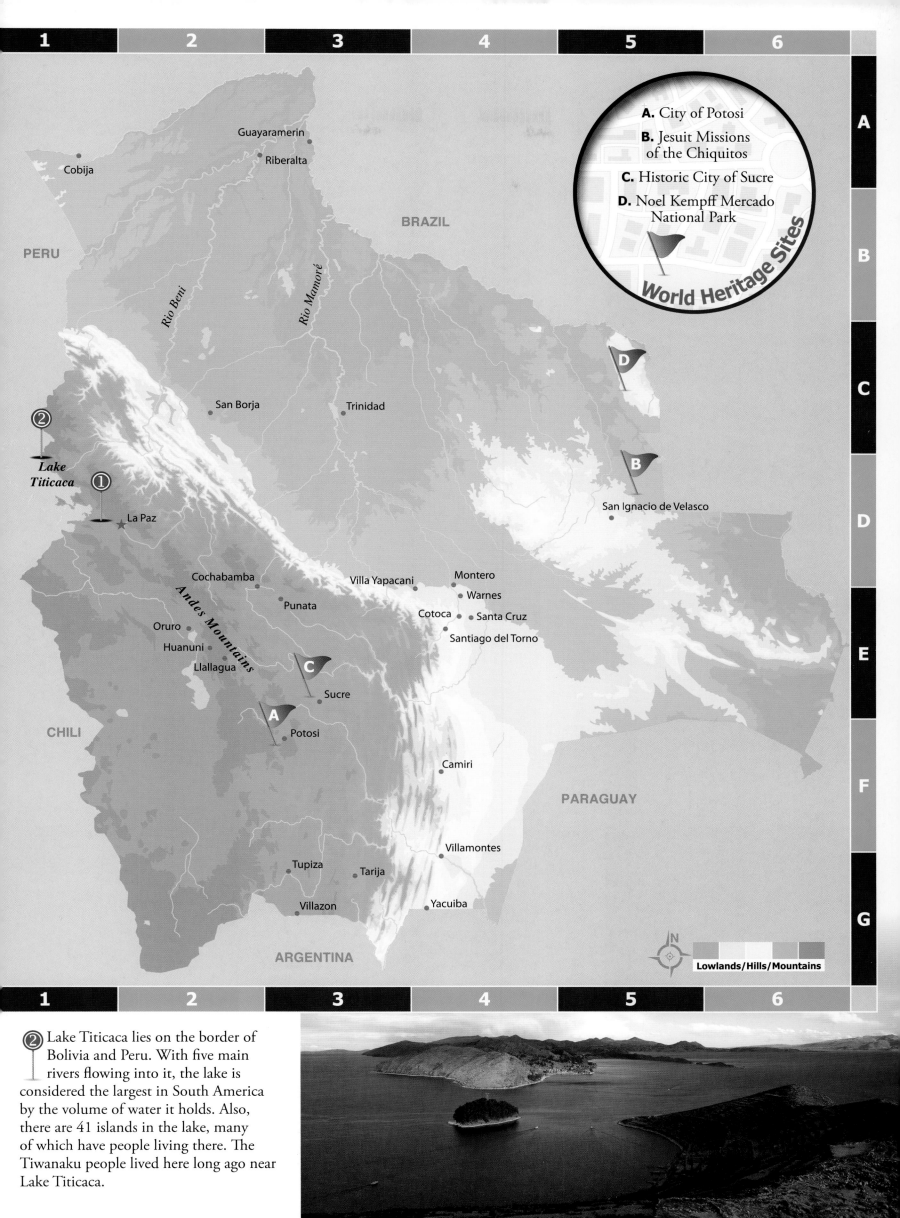

A. City of Potosi

B. Jesuit Missions of the Chiquitos

C. Historic City of Sucre

D. Noel Kempff Mercado National Park

World Heritage Sites

PERU

BRAZIL

Cobija

Guayaramerin

Riberalta

Rio Beni

Rio Mamoré

San Borja

Trinidad

D

②
Lake Titicaca

①
La Paz

B

San Ignacio de Velasco

Cochabamba

Villa Yapacani

Montero

Punata

Warnes

Cotoca
Santa Cruz

Oruro

Andes Mountains

Huanuni

Santiago del Torno

Llallagua

C

Sucre

A

Potosi

CHILI

Camiri

PARAGUAY

Villamontes

Tupiza

Tarija

Yacuiba

Villazon

ARGENTINA

N

Lowlands/Hills/Mountains

② Lake Titicaca lies on the border of Bolivia and Peru. With five main rivers flowing into it, the lake is considered the largest in South America by the volume of water it holds. Also, there are 41 islands in the lake, many of which have people living there. The Tiwanaku people lived here long ago near Lake Titicaca.

EUROPE

Europe is the second smallest continent. It is bordered on the north by the **Arctic Ocean**. The **Ural Mountains** divide it from Asia. To the west is the **Atlantic Ocean**, and to the south, the **Mediterranean Sea**. Europe is also one of the most culturally diverse continents in the world. Each nation has its own distinct culture, history, and language, with about 50 different ones spoken! The European Union (EU) is a group of 27 member nations throughout Europe. The EU unites them economically and politically. It was initially developed by just six countries in 1956 and 1957. Western philosophy and thought spread from Greece throughout ancient European cultures.

① Tulips originally came to the Netherlands from the city now called Istanbul, Turkey, in the middle of the 16th century. The word *tulip* means "turban" in Turkish. However, most people today associate the flower with Holland (another name for the Netherlands).

② Mount Elbrus is the highest mountain on the continent of Europe at 18,510 feet (5,642 meters). The first successful ascent was in 1874. Also known as *Mingi Taw* ("eternal mountain"), it generally takes about a week to summit.

③ The Alps are a mountain range running from southwest France through Switzerland, northern Italy, Austria, and Slovenia. These mountains provide abundant snow for skiers in the cold winter months.

④ The smallest island in the world is Bishop Rock on the western tip of the Isle of Scilly in the United Kingdom. The only building is a lighthouse that is over 160 feet tall.

Vatican City, the center of the Roman Catholic Church, is the smallest independent country in the world. This city-state has a population of just over 800 people. It is located within the city of Rome, Italy.

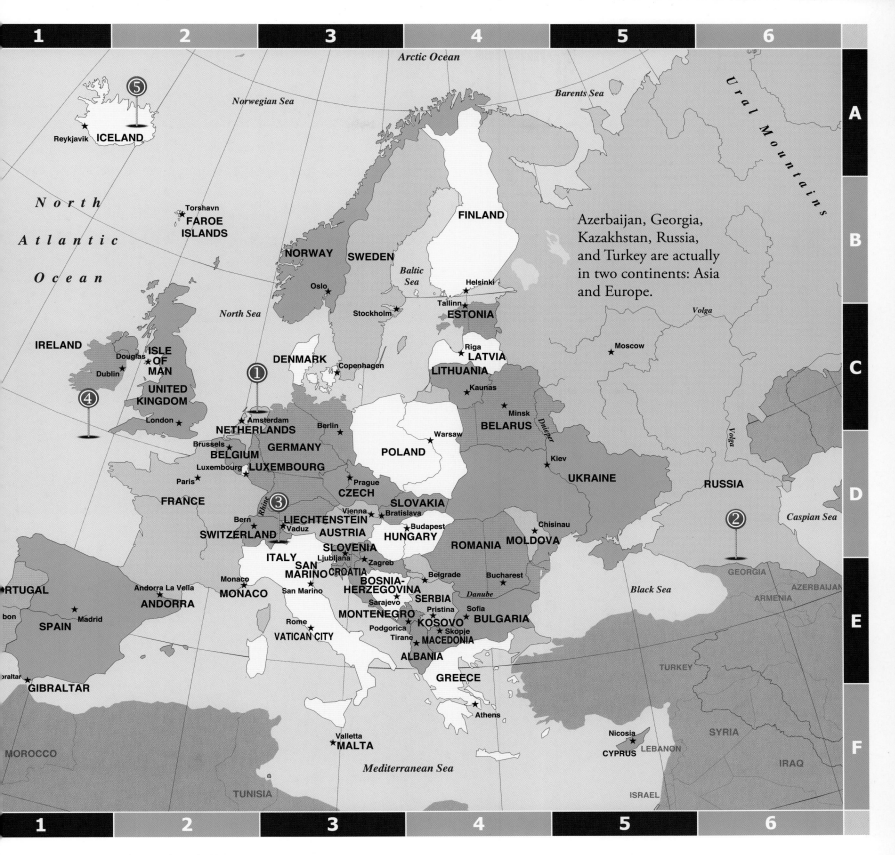

Arctic Ocean

Barents Sea

Ural Mountains

A

Norwegian Sea

⑤ ★ **ICELAND**
Reykjavik

FINLAND

Azerbaijan, Georgia, Kazakhstan, Russia, and Turkey are actually in two continents: Asia and Europe.

B

North

Torshavn *
FAROE ISLANDS

NORWAY **SWEDEN**

Baltic Sea

Volga

Atlantic

Oslo ★

★ Helsinki

C

Ocean

North Sea

Stockholm ★

Tallinn ★
ESTONIA

Moscow ★

IRELAND

Douglas ★
ISLE OF MAN

DENMARK

Copenhagen ★

Riga ★
LATVIA

LITHUANIA

Dublin ★

UNITED KINGDOM

★ Kaunas

Minsk ★

Dnieper

Volga

④

★ Amsterdam
NETHERLANDS

Berlin ★

Warsaw ★

BELARUS

London ★

Brussels ★
BELGIUM

GERMANY

POLAND

D

Luxembourg ★
LUXEMBOURG

Kiev ★

Paris ★

Prague ★
CZECH

UKRAINE

RUSSIA

FRANCE

Rhine

③

Vienna ★ ★ Bratislava
SLOVAKIA

②

Caspian Sea

Bern ★
LIECHTENSTEIN
Vaduz ★

AUSTRIA

★ Budapest

Chisinau ★

GEORGIA

SWITZERLAND

HUNGARY

ROMANIA

MOLDOVA

AZERBAIJAN

SLOVENIA

Ljubljana ★ ★ Zagreb

ARMENIA

ITALY
SAN MARINO

CROATIA

Belgrade ★

Bucharest ★

RTUGAL

Monaco ★
MONACO

San Marino ★

BOSNIA-HERZEGOVINA

Danube

Black Sea

Andorra La Vella ★

Sarajevo ★

SERBIA

Pristina ★

Sofia ★

E

bon ★

Madrid ★
SPAIN

ANDORRA

Rome ★

MONTENEGRO
Podgorica ★

KOSOVO ★ Skopje
Tirane ★ **MACEDONIA**

BULGARIA

TURKEY

VATICAN CITY

ALBANIA

SYRIA

raltar ★
GIBRALTAR

GREECE

Nicosia ★

LEBANON

IRAQ

MOROCCO

Valletta ★
MALTA

Athens ★

CYPRUS

ISRAEL

Mediterranean Sea

F

TUNISIA

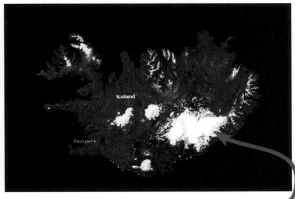

Iceland

Reykjavik

⑤ Europe's largest glacier is named Vatnajökull, and is in the southeast portion of Iceland. Here is Iceland as seen from space, with Vatnajökull appearing as the largest white area to the lower right.

Europe was the birthplace of Western Civilization, laying the foundation for democracy that helps guide and govern many nations still today. The ancient Greek and Roman cultures have forever been connected to biblical history. The Greek language helped the early Christians spread the good news of God's grace throughout the Roman Empire. Many of Paul's letters were directed to churches in Greece and Italy. It was also in Europe that the Protestant Reformation began. Such a rich heritage is spread among the nations, in their history, laws, and cultures.

1611 King James Version Bible ➡

NORWAY

FLAG AND MEANING: It is red with a blue cross outlined in white that extends to the edges of the flag. The vertical part of the cross is shifted to the left side in the style of the Dannebrog (Danish flag). The colors recall Norway's past political unions with Denmark (red and white) and Sweden (blue).

Capital City	Oslo
Government System	Constitutional monarchy
Primary Languages	Bokmal Norwegian, Nynorsk Norwegian
Population	4,707,270
Monetary Unit	Norwegian krone
Area	201,201 sq. miles
National Symbol	Lion
National Anthem	"Ja, vi elsker dette landet" ("Yes, We Love This Country")
Largest City	Oslo 912,046

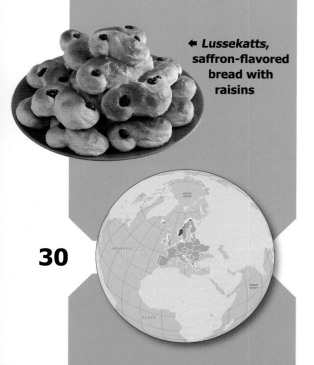

← **Lussekatts, saffron-flavored bread with raisins**

Norway has gone through many changes as a country. For some 400 years they were a part of **Denmark**. They were then ruled by **Sweden** for a time, but worked hard for independence, gaining this in 1905. They have grown stronger economically through oil and gas production starting in the 1960s. The northernmost area of Norway is included in the area referred to as the land of the midnight sun, where the sun does not set from mid-April until mid-August. *Kaamos* is a word that means "polar night" in Finnish. Certain places in Norway experience kaamos from November through the end of January. During this time the sun never rises above the horizon.

Often called *aurora* from a Latin word meaning "dawn," the northern lights are brilliant, colorful displays in the sky. They are found in the Arctic and Antarctic regions of the earth and are caused by charged particles colliding with atoms in the atmosphere.

Along the west coast of Norway there are thousands of fjords or inlets, waterways carved by glaciers at the end of the Ice Age.

Many of the traditional Norwegian clothing styles from the 18th to the 20th centuries are called *bunad*, which simply means "clothing." It can refer to the rural clothing or the folk costumes people wear that are associated with their cultural heritage.

↑ **Urnes Stave Church**

On December 13, Christians in Norway celebrate the festival of St. Lucia. She was killed because of her faith in Christ. Girls are chosen to honor and represent her. They will wear a white dress, red sash, and a wreath garland with candles or lights. Special foods eaten on this day include saffron-flavored bread with raisins, and gingerbread cookies.

Over a thousand years ago, Olav Tryggvason became the first Christian king of Norway. He ruled from A.D. 995 to 1000. However, in trying to make the land a Christian nation he sometimes used methods that we would not consider to be a part of Christ's character. He did have the first church building constructed in his first year as ruler.

Stave churches were first created from wood long ago using similar building styles to those of the Viking people who lived in the region. The Urnes Stave Church was finished around A.D. 1150, and is still standing. This is the oldest wooden church in Norway.

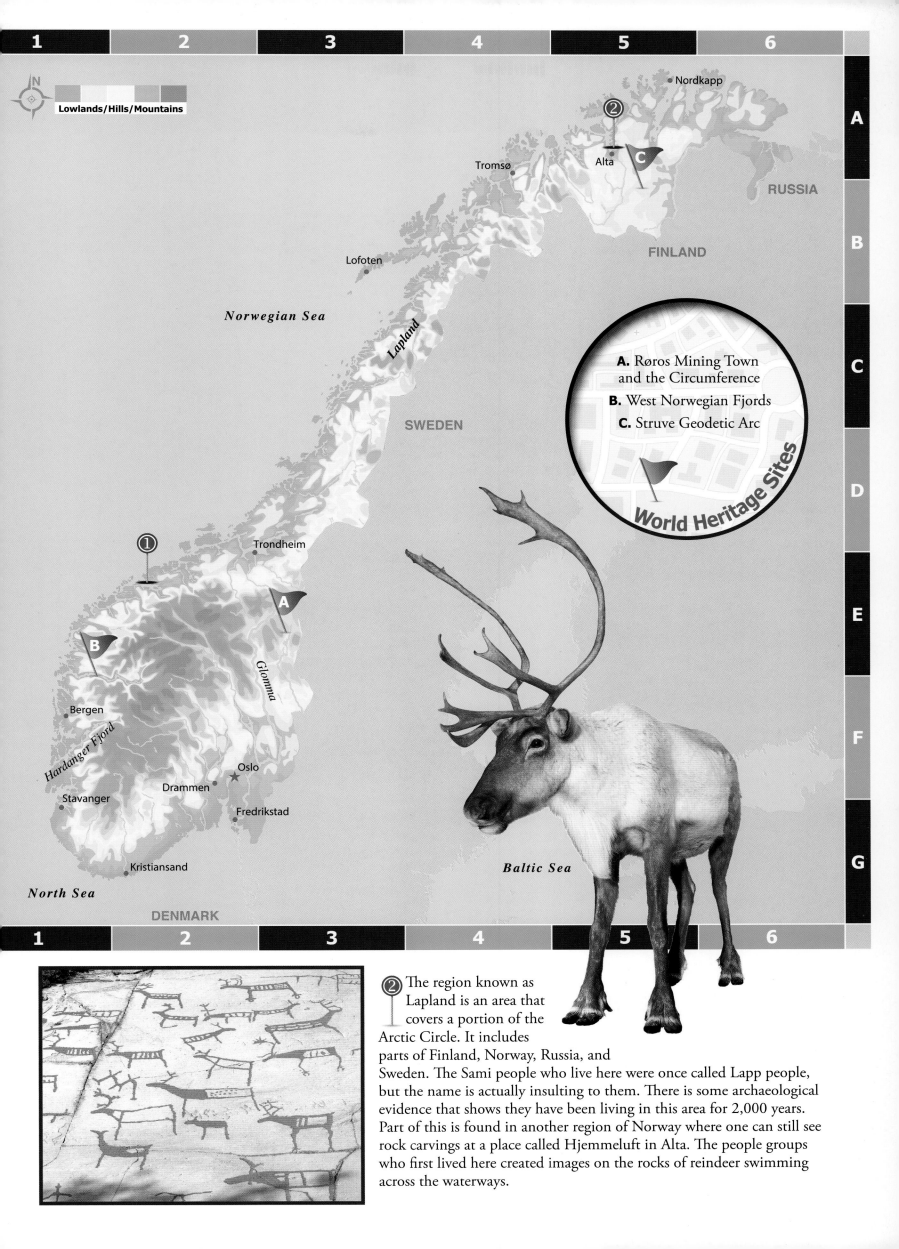

N

Lowlands/Hills/Mountains

Nordkapp

② Alta

C

Tromsø

RUSSIA

FINLAND

Lofoten

Norwegian Sea

Lapland

SWEDEN

A. Røros Mining Town and the Circumference
B. West Norwegian Fjords
C. Struve Geodetic Arc

World Heritage Sites

① Trondheim

A

B

Glomma

Bergen

Hardanger Fjord

Drammen ★ Oslo

Stavanger

Fredrikstad

Baltic Sea

Kristiansand

North Sea

DENMARK

A B C D E F G

② The region known as Lapland is an area that covers a portion of the Arctic Circle. It includes parts of Finland, Norway, Russia, and Sweden. The Sami people who live here were once called Lapp people, but the name is actually insulting to them. There is some archaeological evidence that shows they have been living in this area for 2,000 years. Part of this is found in another region of Norway where one can still see rock carvings at a place called Hjemmeluft in Alta. The people groups who first lived here created images on the rocks of reindeer swimming across the waterways.

FLAG AND MEANING: There are three equal vertical bands of green, white, and red. The design was inspired by the French flag brought to Italy by Napoleon in 1797. The colors are those of Milan (red and white) combined with the green uniform color of the Milanese civic guard.

Capital City	Rome
Government System	Republic
Primary Languages	Italian, German, French, and Slovene
Population	61,261,254
Monetary Unit	Euro
Area	187,243 sq. miles
National Symbol	White, five-pointed star (Stella d'Italia)
National Anthem	"Il Canto degli Italiani" ("The Song of the Italians")
Largest City	Rome 2,193,030

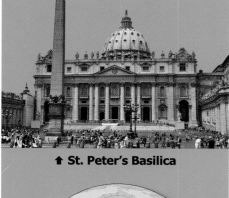

↑ **St. Peter's Basilica**

Italy's unique, boot-shaped land is nearly surrounded by the waters of the **Mediterranean Sea**. **Sardinia** and **Sicily** are also a part of Italy; two of the largest islands that help make up this great nation. Its history is rich and vast, dating back thousands of years. The capital city of Rome was a center of civilization at the time of Christ. Surviving numerous invasions, Italy became the birthplace of the Renaissance movement that inspired art, philosophy, and more.

Renaissance is a word that means "rebirth." One name at the center of the Italian Renaissance movement was the architect, engineer, inventor, musician, painter, sculptor, and writer Leonardo da Vinci. His incredible talent has left us the legacy of such paintings as *The Last Supper* and the *Mona Lisa*. He was also very inventive and ahead of his time. His drawings and notes discussed such possible inventions as a helicopter and a tank.

① The only active volcanoes in the mainland portion of Europe are found in Italy. The tectonic plates of Africa and Europe meet near here and magma is forced up by the pressure. In the last 100 years, three of Italy's volcanoes have erupted. These volcanoes are Mount Etna on Sicily, Mount Vesuvius near Naples, and Stromboli, an Aeolian island that is located off the western coast of Italy.

St. Peter's Basilica was originally built in the fourth century to hold the disciple's tomb. Today it is considered perhaps the greatest church building in all of Christianity, with designs by artists such as Michelangelo. These buildings are part of Vatican City within Rome, which is considered the smallest sovereign city-state in the world.

Constantine the Great ruled as emperor of the Roman Empire from A.D. 306 to 337. The first Roman emperor to embrace the Christian faith, he made it the official religion. Though he was a powerful military leader, his faith was at best mingled with former pagan practices. The city of Constantinople was named in his honor.

LEONARDO DA VINCI

For thousands of years, swordfish have been eaten in Italy. They are often caught between the island of Sicily and the main coastline. These fish actually use their "swords" to slash their prey to be able to catch them.

The Colosseum stands in the center of Rome as an amazing example of engineering and construction. Completed in A.D. 80, it could seat around 50,000 people. Gladiators once fought here, and there were also animal hunts and public executions of Christians. It is considered by some as a shrine to the Christian faith.

Lowlands/Hills/Mountains

AUSTRIA

SWITZERLAND

SOLVENIA

Trento

Aosta

Milan

Verona

A

Venice

Trieste

Padova

CROATIA

Po River

Turin

Genova

Bologna

RANCE

Arno River

Florence

Ancona

Tiber River

C

Perugia

Adriatic Sea

Corsica

L'Aquila

Rome

Campobasso

Bari

Napoli

Potenza

Mount
Vesuvius

Taranto

Sardinia

Tyrrhenian Sea

Cagliari

①

Catanzaro

B

Stromboli

Messina

①

Palermo

Mediterranean Sea

Mount Etna

Sicily

Catania

TUNISIA

ALGERIA

A. Botanical Garden
(Orto Botanico), Padua

B. Isole Eolie (Aeolian Islands)

C. Assisi, the Basilica of San
Francesco and
Other Franciscan Sites

World Heritage Sites

Capital City	Paris
Government System	Republic
Primary Languages	French
Population	65,630,692
Monetary Unit	Euro
Area	400,039 sq. miles
National Symbol	Gallic rooster
National Anthem	"La Marseillaise" ("The Song of Marseille")
Largest City	Paris 2,193,030

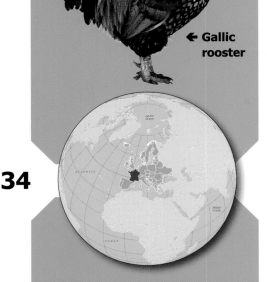

← Gallic rooster

The roots of France go back more than 2,000 years. **Paris**, the capital city, was a small fishing village approximately 200 years before Christ. This people group was known by the name *Parisii*. France has become a country that leads the way in fashion, food, and cultural trends. The beautiful coastlines and castles, as well as the delicious cuisine and winter sports in the **French Alps** draw over 75 million visitors a year. It is the most-visited country in the world.

① The Musée Rodin in Paris first opened in 1919. The focus of this remarkable museum is the works of Auguste Rodin, a French sculptor. One finds many large statues in wide open spaces and beautiful settings outside, as well as the indoor gallery. Many go to see the statue garden that is set in a wondrous park setting. The museum receives 700,000 people annually to view the collection of 6,600 sculptures, 8,000 drawings, and thousands of other photographs and art pieces. Rodin donated his entire collection so people could experience his works, including his famous statue, *The Thinker*.

② In 1940, the caves of Lascaux were discovered by several French teens exploring. Here they found walls covered in colorful paintings of birds, bulls, horses, reindeer, and more. Symbols and signs are mingled with the animals and people sketched on stone by early settlers of this region.

John Calvin was born in France in the year 1509. He became an influential theologian of the Protestant Reformation and left a powerful legacy through his work, as well as commentaries on many of the biblical books. His work helped form the religious principles for some Christian denominations.

Born in 475 in Lyon, Burgundy, France, Clotilde was influential in bringing her husband, King Clovis I to Christianity. Prior to this his family had worshiped many "gods," and the king was no exception. Because of his great love for Clotilde, he was baptized on Christmas Day 496, and they soon after made Paris the capital city of their kingdom.

The Salvation Army was begun by William Booth in England. His daughter, Catherine (Katie) Booth, brought this ministry to the poor, hungry, and homeless of Paris. She preached the Gospel in the streets, even though people often threw rocks and mud at her. Today the Salvation Army continues its international ministry to improve the lives of people.

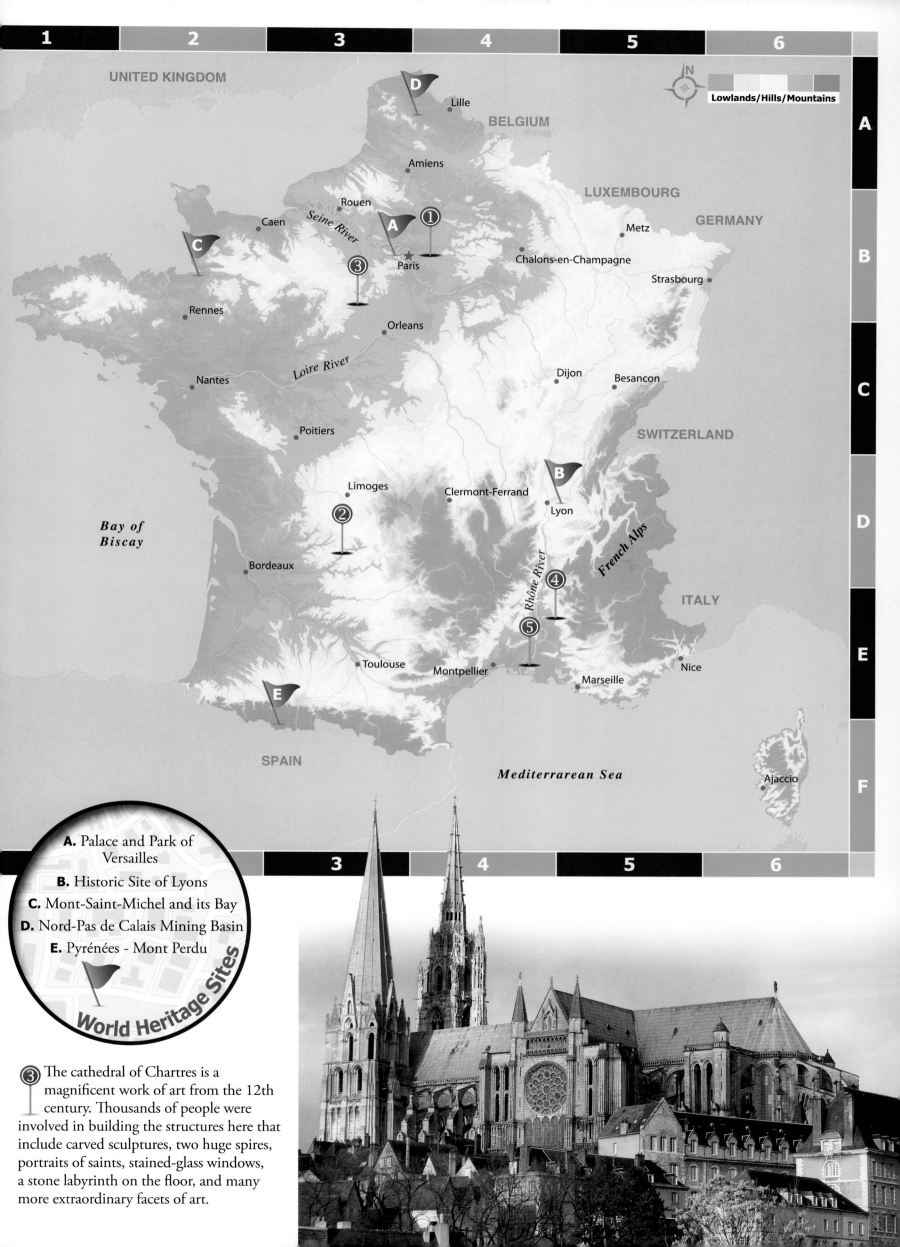

Lowlands/Hills/Mountains

UNITED KINGDOM

BELGIUM

LUXEMBOURG

GERMANY

D

Lille

Amiens

Rouen

Caen

Seine River

A ①

Metz

Chalons-en-Champagne

Strasbourg

C

③

Paris

Rennes

Orleans

Dijon

Besancon

Nantes

Loire River

SWITZERLAND

Poitiers

Bay of Biscay

Limoges

②

Clermont-Ferrand

B

Lyon

French Alps

Bordeaux

Rhône River

④

ITALY

⑤

Toulouse

Montpellier

Marseille

Nice

E

SPAIN

Mediterrarean Sea

Ajaccio

A
B
C
D
E
F

A. Palace and Park of Versailles

B. Historic Site of Lyons

C. Mont-Saint-Michel and its Bay

D. Nord-Pas de Calais Mining Basin

E. Pyrénées - Mont Perdu

World Heritage Sites

③ The cathedral of Chartres is a magnificent work of art from the 12th century. Thousands of people were involved in building the structures here that include carved sculptures, two huge spires, portraits of saints, stained-glass windows, a stone labyrinth on the floor, and many more extraordinary facets of art.

First held in 1903, the Tour de France bicycle race is perhaps the most significant yearly sporting event that takes place in the country, occurring every July. While routes change each year, the riders still face such challenges as the difficult mountain stages in the Pyrenees and the Alps. French cyclists have won the race more than any other country in a race history that has been uninterrupted, with the exception of two world wars.

↑ Roads along Pyrenees Mountains

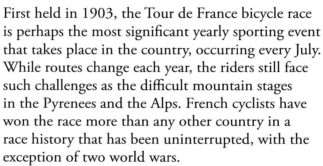

From 350 to 400 different kinds of cheeses are produced, with many of the specialty cheese varieties named after a particular town or region in France, such as Brie and Camembert.

A special day is set aside on the last Sunday of June to honor mothers with gifts and treats. One such treat that is eaten is called Gâteaux, a small cake often served hot with a delicious cream filling.

France celebrates its independence on July 14 during what is known as Bastille Day, or in France as La Fête Nationale. A military parade has been part of the celebrations since 1880. The parade route is along the Champs-Élysées from the Arc de Triomphe to the Place de la Concorde.

Each region of France is very distinct, but one aspect of life they have in common is the love of great food. No matter what regional favorite is being served, lively outdoor cafes and restaurants allow people to sit and enjoy the beauty of the cities and surrounding areas. Considered by many to have some of the most delicious foods found anywhere in the world, even the smallest cafes can require reservations because of their popularity with local diners and tourists.

← The Caravans
— Gypsy Camp near Arles

There are approximately 15,000 Roma gypsies in France. They have a rich heritage, going back hundreds of years to northern India. From there they dispersed across Europe and other parts of the world. They are a very supportive community of people; however, they are facing increasing persecution in France because of prejudice. Some have been forced from the country or left for parts of Britain seeking employment and stability. The painter Vincent van Gogh had a deep love and respect for the Romani people. His painting made near Arles depicts their nomadic life as it was in 1888.

Lavendula, more commonly known as lavender, is a plant that grows throughout southern Europe as well as parts of Africa, the Mediterranean, Asia, and India. Though in some places in the world it is considered a weed, here in France it is grown commercially and sold. It has been used to develop a specialized honey flavor, and its oils are used as a scent in soaps and other household products.

④ The Ancient Theatre of Orange is of Roman construction and was built during the first century A.D. in southern France. Sites like the theater were used as a way of spreading culture throughout the Roman Empire. Festivities at the site were free of charge to the public and events included poetry readings and comedy plays. The theater was officially closed in A.D. 391.

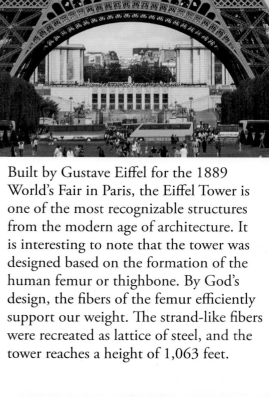

Nuclear power is the primary source of electricity in France, and the country is a world leader in the use of this nuclear technology. With few natural sources for energy and in an effort to reduce its need for foreign oil, the country continued its research into nuclear energy, which began around the turn of the 20th century. The nation's first nuclear power plant began operation in 1962.

⑤ Provence is the area of southeastern France next to Italy and bordering the Mediterranean Sea. Within Provence, you will find the Camargue, a large river delta surrounded entirely by reed-filled marshes. The area is well known for the hundreds of birds that live here. It is one of the few habitats in Europe for the greater flamingo.

Built by Gustave Eiffel for the 1889 World's Fair in Paris, the Eiffel Tower is one of the most recognizable structures from the modern age of architecture. It is interesting to note that the tower was designed based on the formation of the human femur or thighbone. By God's design, the fibers of the femur efficiently support our weight. The strand-like fibers were recreated as lattice of steel, and the tower reaches a height of 1,063 feet.

FLAG AND MEANING: The German flag is made up of three equal horizontal stripes of black, red, and gold. The colors hold significance in Germanic history. This design relates back to the banner of the Holy Roman Emperor. It displayed a black eagle with red claws and beak on top of a golden background.

Capital city	Berlin
Government System	Federal republic
Primary Languages	German
Population	81,305,856
Monetary unit	Euro
Area	221,843 sq. miles
National symbol	Black eagle ➡
National anthem	"Lied der Deutschen" ("Song of the Germans")
Largest City	Berlin 3,460,725

According to the U.S. census, 15 percent of Americans claim to be of German descent. This is the largest ancestry group among the U.S. population, even more than British.

From before the time of Christ, this land was called Germania by none other than the fierce dictator of the Roman Empire, Julius Caesar. Comprised of 16 states, Germany has provided a thriving place for composers, artists, reformers, and inventors for hundreds of years. The current nation was formed in 1990 from a reunification of the eastern German Democratic Republic and the western Federal Republic of Germany. The country had been divided since the end of World War II. The landscape is shaped by the lowlands in the north, the uplands in the center, and the **Bavarian Alps** to the south. This diversity provides rich resources of coal, copper, iron ore, natural gas, nickel, salt, timber, uranium, and more.

Cars are able to travel at speeds of 150 to 200 miles per hour on Germany's autobahn. The autobahn is an abbreviated form of *Bundesautobahn*, which simply means "federal highway."

In 1456, Johannes Gutenberg (c. 1398–1468) printed the Bible in Mainz, Germany, in a version of late 4th-century Latin. The moveable type printing press he developed would make Scripture widely available. Before this, each copy had to be made by hand, which meant that only the rich had direct access to God's Word.

Martin Luther (1483–1546) began translating the Bible into the German language in 1521. People would then be able to read God's Word in their native language. This would help transform the world through the Protestant Reformation period. One of the Reformation's refrains was *Sola Gratia*, meaning we are saved by God's grace alone.

Johann Sebastian Bach (1685–1750), one of the greatest composers of the Western world, sought God's glory through the music he created. He often wrote *SDG* (*Soli Deo Gloria*, "To God alone be glory") at the end of his musical compositions. Another composer, George Frideric Handel, also gave glory to God for his work.

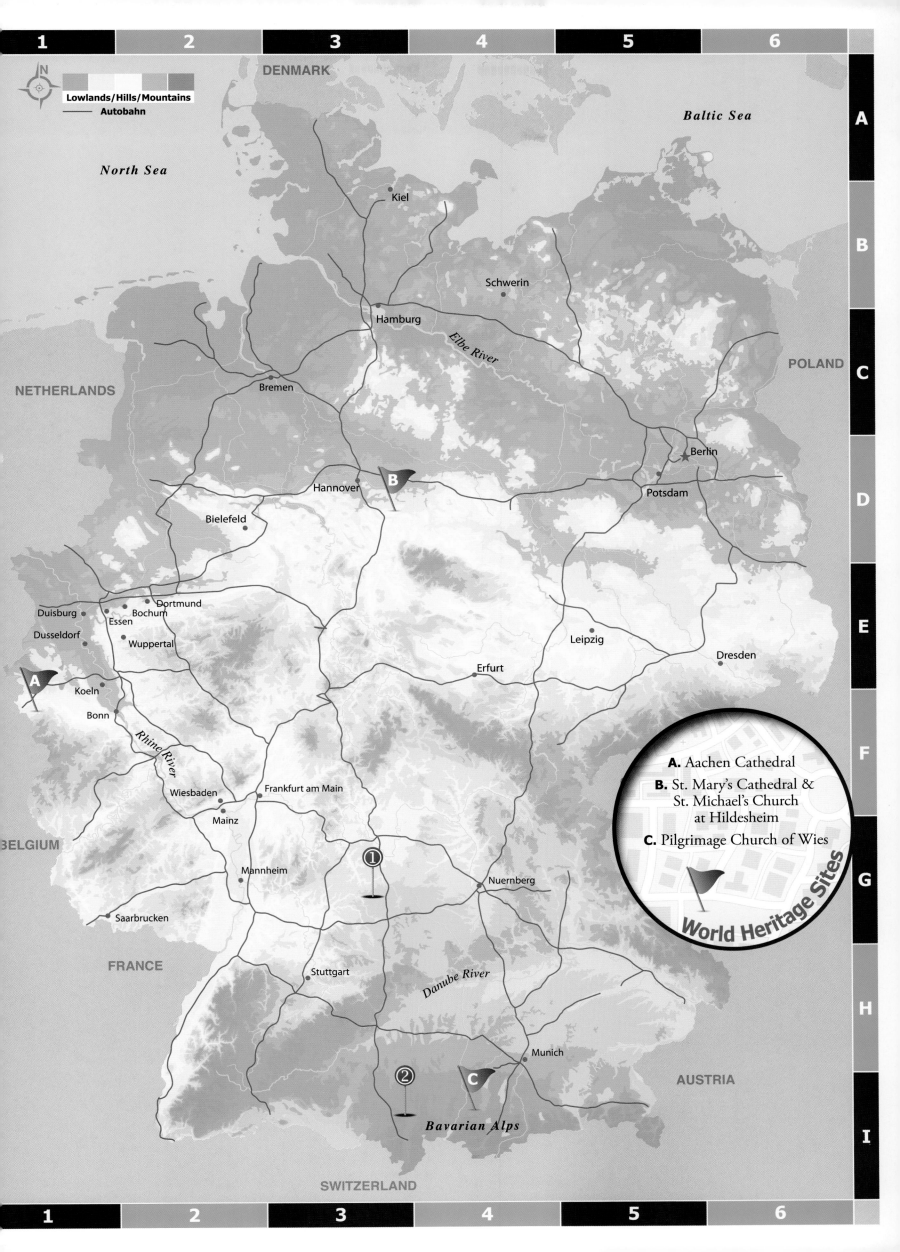

Nearly 30 percent of the country is covered by forests. In southwestern Germany, the Black Forest is so thick with trees that it is difficult for light to reach the forest floor.

Christmas is a holiday set aside by Christians around the world to honor the birth of Christ. It is often celebrated on December 25, though it begins on the 24th in Germany where it is called *Weihnachten*. Christmas history runs deep in Germany where many of the Christmas tree traditions are often linked to Martin Luther in the 16th century.

Today, customs include singing carols, giving gifts, attending special church services, and eating holiday foods. These include spiced fruitcakes called *stollen*, and a fruitbread made from fruits, nuts, and seeds called *früchtebrot*.

Christmas fairs and markets are plentiful beginning the last week of November and going through Christmas Eve. Here one finds hand-crafted gifts and toys, as well as delicious sweets of the season, such as gingerbread and marzipan. Such treats play a part in *The Nutcracker and the Mouse King* by German author E.T.A. Hoffman. His book was adapted by Russian composer Pyotr Ilyich Tchaikovsky for "The Nutcracker," perhaps the most famous ballet in the world.

40

① Rothenburg ob der Tauber, famous historical town

The Rhine Valley, Lorch ➡

Rivers are a diverse ecosystem or habitat. The strength of the current, the temperature of the water, the amount of oxygen, and many other factors create the differences between these areas on earth. Millions of people get their drinking water from the **Rhine.** It had become quite polluted, but much has been done to clean it up and allow salmon and other fish to thrive again.

The world's fresh water is kept pure through the water cycle. Rainfall and snowfall cover the earth with fresh sources of water. These often soak into the ground or are channeled through rivers that empty into lakes. Eventually the waters in streams and rivers empty into the sea where the cycle repeats.

In the summer, large lakes are layered with warm water on top, and a cold layer of about 39°F on the bottom. The warm, lighter water tends to remain above the cold, denser or heavier water. Virtually no mixing of the layers above or below that certain line occurs. That deprives the upper layer of nutrients and the bottom layer of oxygen. In the fall, cooling of surface waters causes them to sink to the bottom. This mixing of the water layers creates a circulation of oxygen and surge of nutrients. The process is called an overturn. In the spring, a warming of the icy surface water again causes the temperature layers to form. A second overturn then occurs. Many beautiful effects result from God's design of rivers and waterways.

② There are literally hundreds of castles spread across the landscape of Germany. One of the most famous in the world is the Neuschwanstein Castle. The castle was built on a hill overlooking the village of Hohenschwangau. Ludwig II of Bavaria had it built as a place to relax from his duties. After his death in 1886, this exquisite palace opened its doors to the public. The name means "New Swan Stone," and comes from Richard Wagner's opera character, the Sun Knight.

Sausages are made from chopped up meat mixed with herbs and spices, then pressed into a casing. Germany has well over a thousand varieties! These include bratwurst, frankfurters, and Landjäger.

German Shepherd dogs were first bred in Germany in 1899 by a retired military man, Max Emil Frederich von Stephanitz. He found a dog that he thought fit his perfect description of a work dog, and named him Horand von Grafrath. His dog is the first German Shepherd added to the breed's official registry. Raised to guard sheep initially, now they are often used as guard dogs and for search and rescue missions.

FLAG AND MEANING: A blue field shows the red cross of Saint George (patron saint of England) edged in white and added to the diagonal red cross of Saint Patrick (patron saint of Ireland). The diagonal white cross of Saint Andrew (patron saint of Scotland) is also included. The flag is properly known as the Union Flag, but commonly called the Union Jack.

Capital City	London
Government System	Constitutional monarchy and Commonwealth realm
Primary Languages	English, Scots, Scottish Gaelic, Welsh, Irish, and Cornish.
Population	63,047,162
Monetary Unit	British pound
Area	151,372 sq. miles
National Symbol	Lion (England); lion, unicorn (Scotland); red dragon (Wales); harp (Northern Ireland)
National Anthem	"God Save the Queen"; alternate is King, when the ruler is male
Largest City	London 7,172,091

The United Kingdom is a nation that includes the countries of **England**, **Scotland**, and **Wales** (these three are sometimes called Great Britain), as well as **Northern Ireland**. It was once said that the sun never set on the British Empire, primarily because of its many colonies and territories around the globe. This once included portions of the United States, Canada, India, and Australia, as well as many other territories. It has been a center for Western civilization and Christian thought for over 1,000 years.

Often called football, soccer is considered by many to be the world's most popular sport. Team games played with a ball and goals have been known since before the time of Christ. The ancient Romans played *harpastum* and in China something similar was called *cuju*. Its roots in England go as far back as the eighth century!

The Old Course at **St. Andrews** in St. Andrews, Fife, Scotland, is considered by many to be the oldest golf course in the world. Golf was first played here back in the early 1400s. Just as it was gaining popularity, James II of Scotland banned the game, wanting young men to focus more on their archery skills!

The influence of William Shakespeare on the English language and literature can hardly be exaggerated. His life spanned A.D. 1564 to 1616 and he made a name for himself as a poet and playwright. Creating such memorable works as "Romeo and Juliet" and "Hamlet," he has become the most-quoted author of the English-speaking world. Because of this, many of the words and phrases he used or coined are still in use today. His plays are still studied and performed.

William Wilberforce spent much of his life fighting against the slave trade throughout the British Empire. He realized this destructive practice left a horrid stain on the Christian heritage of his nation. By his direct efforts, the slave trade was outlawed in the United Kingdom in 1807 and slavery ended in 1833.

King James I of England commissioned an English Bible translation in A.D. 1604. Completed in 1611 by 54 translators, it came to be called the Authorized Version in 1814. Filled with poetic prose, this has become the most popular English version of the Bible, with an estimated one billion copies sold. It is referred to as the King James Version or KJV.

Dating back to A.D. 597, a monk named Augustine came to Canterbury to serve. This was called establishing his seat or "cathedra," and so a cathedral was built. Since then many people have traveled to this place for over 1,400 years, often to pray. Almost 2,000 services are held yearly in this beautiful building built to the glory of God.

World Heritage Sites

A. Dorset and East Devon Coast

B. Maritime Greenwich

C. Castles and Town Walls of King Edward in Gwynedd

① Thousands of puffins flock to Scotland's coastlines. These wonderfully colorful birds can fill their beaks with many small fish. They often do this from late April to mid-August when they bring the fish to feed their young. Some of the places to watch them are the **Treshnish Isles**, the **Isle of May**, and the **Farne Islands**.

SCOTLAND

Aberdeen

River Tay

① **Treshnich Isles**

St. Andrews

① **Isle of May**

Atlantic Ocean

Glasgow

Edinburgh

④

① **Farne Islands**

North Sea

Newcastle upon Tyne

Durham

NORTHERN IRELAND

Belfast

IRELAND

Leeds

Kingston upon Hull

C Liverpool

Manchester

Sheffield

⑥

Derby   Nottingham

River Severn

Birmingham

Coventry

WALES

ENGLAND

B

Caerdydd

Bristol   Reading

River Thames

London

③

⑤

②

BELGIUM

Southampton

A

Plymouth

English Channel

FRANCE

N

Lowlands/Hills/Mountains
------ Country border
——— Channel Tunnel

A
B
C
D
E
F
G
H
I

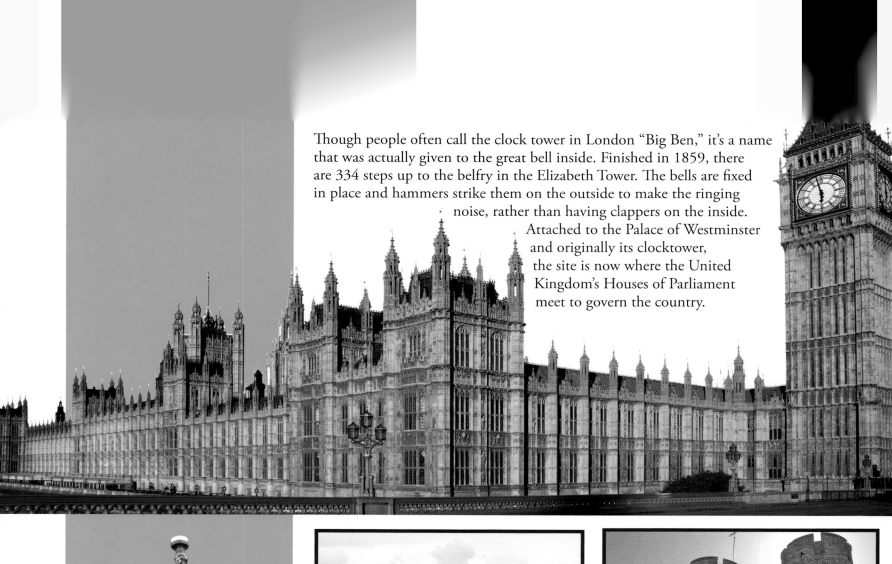

Though people often call the clock tower in London "Big Ben," it's a name that was actually given to the great bell inside. Finished in 1859, there are 334 steps up to the belfry in the Elizabeth Tower. The bells are fixed in place and hammers strike them on the outside to make the ringing noise, rather than having clappers on the inside. Attached to the Palace of Westminster and originally its clocktower, the site is now where the United Kingdom's Houses of Parliament meet to govern the country.

Scottish lakes, or *lochs*, are a familiar feature in the landscape. Some estimate over 31,000 freshwater lakes are found throughout Scotland, though most are in the Highland region. The term *loch* can also refer to a fjord. While Loch Ness is famous for sightings of an unknown creature, Loch Lomond and the Trossachs National Park is one of the first national parks in Scotland, and is the second largest in the U.K.

◄ Bagpipes and traditional Scottish clothing are closely associated with the Highlands of Scotland. This mountainous region includes Ben Nevis, the highest mountain, formed from the collapsed dome of a volcano. The Highlands were home to regional groups of people who created clothing from local dyes and by weavers in patterns unique to them. Scottish tartan designs are called plaids in other countries. The bagpipe has reed pipes that are played by squeezing air from the flexible bag with your arm.

The Canterbury Tales was first printed in 1475. Written by Geoffrey Chaucer, it describes the stories of pilgrims coming to the cathedral. The word "canter" originated from the pace of the pilgrims' horses as they came upon the cathedral.

Sometimes called the Chunnel, the Channel Tunnel transports passengers under ground and sea from Folkestone, Kent, in the United Kingdom to Coquelles near Calais in France. This rail tunnel is over 31 miles long and goes underneath the English Channel. That makes it the longest undersea tunnel in the world.

③ The White Cliffs of Dover are an important geographic landmark on the coastline of Great Britain. White chalk and streaks of black flint form the distinctive coloring on the cliffs, which rise 350 feet above the water. Facing the mainland of Europe, the site is unstable, with erosion wearing away the soft chalk. The cliffs can even be seen from the coast of France on clear days.

④ The Giants Causeway is an area in Northern Ireland with 40,000 interlocking columns of basalt, a rock formed by rapid cooling of volcanic lava. Most columns are hexagonal, but others are found with anywhere from four to eight sides. Discovered in 1692, the area has rock formations which have been weathered, a process of being altered or broken down through forces like wind and water. The Giants Causeway is also home to a variety of sea birds and unusual plants.

Similar to a fruit cake, Bara Brith or speckled bread is a favorite in Wales. It is yeast bread with spices, tea, and candied or dried fruits added.

← Snowdon beetle

⑤ The purpose behind the massive stacked stones of Stonehenge was considered quite a mystery until the 20th century. An astronomer, Sir Norman Lockyer, began to see correlations between the way the stones were placed and their alignment with the angles of the sun, moon, and stars as they cross the sky. This remarkable structure was a detailed calendar from several thousand years ago! Still being studied today, the site continues to reveal archaeological mysteries.

⑥ Snowdonia National Park is the first and largest national park in Wales. It is named for Snowdon, the highest mountain in Wales at 3,560 feet. In addition to the mountains, the area's coastline is a protected area. This park is home to rare species of mammals and birds, the only place in the U.K. where some unusual plants and insects, like the Snowdon beetle, can be found.

FLAG AND MEANING: It has three equal horizontal bands of white, blue, and red. The colors may have been based on those of the Dutch flag; despite many popular interpretations, there is no official meaning assigned to the colors of the Russian flag.

Capital City	Moscow
Government System	Federation
Primary Languages	Russian
Population	142,517,670
Monetary Unit	Russian ruble
Area	10,624,355 sq. miles
National Symbol	Bear; double-headed eagle
National Anthem	"Gimn Rossiyskoy Federatsii" ("National Anthem of the Russian Federation")
Largest City	Moscow 11,514,330

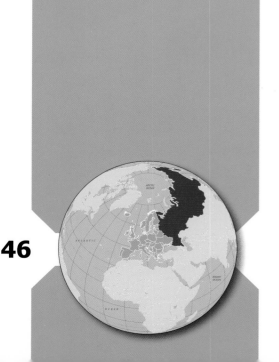

Russia is by far the largest country in the world; nearly twice the size of Canada, the next largest by square miles. It is actually one of the few countries to be in two continents. Russia used to be a part of a nation called the U.S.S.R. (Union of Soviet Socialist Republics). Formed in 1922, just five years after the Russian Revolution, it consisted of 15 countries. The U.S.S.R. was broken up in 1991 after a series of anti-Communist revolutions throughout eastern Europe. The cold northern region of Russia is called *Siberia*, which means "sleeping land" in the Turkic language. The two summits of Mount Elbrus, a dormant volcano in the **Caucasus Mountains**, mark the highest point in Russia, with both over 18,400 feet.

The longest rail system in the world is the **Trans-Siberian Railway**. It connects Moscow in the west with Vladivostok on the east, running over 5,770 miles! The journey takes about eight days and crosses seven time zones! It was built between 1891 and 1916, and portions of it even cross through China.

1 The Ural Mountains are more than just a boundary between Europe and Asia. The mountains have been a rich source of iron and copper ores, as well as gemstones and minerals. Extending over 1,600 miles, the mountain range is divided into five areas — polar, sub-arctic, Northern, Central, and Southern sections. The tallest mountain in the range is Mount Narodnaya.

2 Geysers are hot springs that send tall spouts of water or steam into the air. They are found in only a few places around the world. Within the Kamchatka Peninsula, you can find the large Valley of the Geysers. Filled with thermal springs and around 90 geysers, the area is an interesting mix of hot and cold, with the hot and watery valley contrasting the snow-covered hills and landscape.

The Solovyetsky Islands in the White Sea of northern Russia is home to the Solovyetsky Monastery. This collection of buildings includes the Uspenskaya Church, built in the 16th century. Over the last few hundred years, it has served as church, fort, and prison. The remarkable domes are similar to St. Basil's Cathedral in Moscow.

On April 12, 1961, Yuri Gagarin became the first person in space. His ship, *Vostok 1*, helped him circle the earth for one hour and 48 minutes. Contrary to rumors, he never stated that he didn't see God when he was in space. He and his family were members of the Orthodox Church in Russia.

The Russian Synodal Bible was the first full Bible translation of the Scriptures into the Russian language. Though it was started in 1813, the entire Bible was not completed until 1876. It is read by the Russian Orthodox Church, many Protestant churches, and Roman Catholics in Russia.

Lowlands/Hills/Mountains
Trans-Siberian Railway

Arctic Ocean

Norwegian Sea

FINLAND
A
Saint Petersburg
①
C
Moscow
Nizhniy Novgorod
Voronezh
Kazan
Perm
Saratov
Samara
Ufa
Yekaterinburg
Volgograd
Chelyabinsk
Omsk
Novosibirsk
Krasnoyarsk
③
Blagoveschensk
CHINA
Vladivostok
B
MONGOLIA
KAZAKHSTAN
Caspian Sea
Volga
Ural
Ural Mountains
Ob
Norilsk
Kara Sea
Laptev Sea
East Siberian Sea
②
Kamchatka Peninsula
Sea of Okhotsk
JAPAN
ucasus
untains
AINE
ARUS

St. Basil's Cathedral is a landmark in **Moscow** in famous Red Square, with a rich history of both architecture and changing attitudes by those in power about Christianity. Constructed by order of Tsar Ivan IV Vasilyech (known as Ivan the Terrible) from 1555 to 1561, the cathedral was built as a monument to military victories. Its colorful onion-shaped domes were first painted in 1680. The original building complex included a central church surrounded by eight others, with a tenth church over the grave of St. Basil. Originally celebrated as an earthly symbol of heaven, by 1929 the anti-Christian communist government confiscated and closed the building as a church.

A. Historic Centre of Saint Petersburg and Related Groups of Monuments
B. Golden Mountains of Altai
C. Church of the Ascension, Kolomenskoye

World Heritage Sites

With an interest in shipping, Tsar Peter the Great in 1703 decided that Russia needed a good seaport. After capturing a strategic section of land, he laid the foundations of the city that would eventually become known as **St. Petersburg**. The city was built by prisoners of war and poor workers, or peasants, from throughout Russia. The city was the official capital from 1712 to 1728, when it was reverted back to Moscow. In 1732, Empress Anna of Russia changed the capital back to St. Petersburg, where it would remain until the Russian revolution in 1917.

Large countries have multiple time zones. Russia alone covers 11 time zones and is located in two continents: Europe and Asia. More than 70 percent of the people live in the European portion, but nearly 75 percent of Russia's land is in Asia.

③ Lake Baikal in southern Russia is the deepest lake in the world. Its deepest point is 5,387 feet (1,642 meters). It is also the largest freshwater lake in the world by volume.

The nerpa or Baikal seal is found only in the waters of Lake Baikal in Siberia. This true seal (or earless seal, to classify it among different types of others) is an important part of the ecosystem of the lake. By feeding on a fish called *golomyanka*, also found only in Lake Baikal, the seals help to keep the population numbers of this rapidly reproducing fish down. Mothers care for newborns for two and a half months, which is longer than seals do elsewhere. Nerpa seals can live to be over 50 years of age and can stay under water for over an hour if needed.

The Siberian or Amur tiger can be found mainly in the mountain regions of Russia. It is thought that there are only about 400 tigers that still live here, so many people and organizations are trying to protect them. These beautiful animals can reach up to 1,000 pounds! Because of their size, they have been known to kill and eat brown and black bears, though they mainly feed on red deer and wild boars.

Siberia is a geographic area east of the Ural Mountains, to the Arctic Ocean in the north, and south to the border of China. Almost 80 percent of Russia is within Siberia. Rich in minerals, oil, and gas reserves, it is a region where agriculture is difficult because of a short growing season. Reindeer are raised in herds here, and Siberia has vast forests, which are being logged as an industry. Fishing is another strong industry because of the fish-rich waters of the Sea of Okhotsk. Much of Siberia does not have roads and so must rely on trains for transport.

The arctic tundra is a permanently frozen landscape. The term *tundra* comes from a Finnish word that means "barren land," though there are arctic fox, beavers, snowy owls, and more that live here. Because the land is frozen, few if any trees can grow. Often only mosses and lichen can establish roots. Approximately one-tenth of Russia is tundra with this poor, marshy soil. In the summer months when there is a slight thaw, many birds flock to the area and feed on the bugs that thrive during that time. There are actually three different kinds of tundra. First, there is the arctic tundra with mostly bare land. Next is the shrubby tundra with small plants, including short birch and willow trees. Finally, there is the wooded tundra with slightly larger birch and spruce trees.

Russian nesting dolls, also called *matryoshka* dolls, are wooden dolls that can be placed one inside the next. Each is slightly smaller than the one before. Vasily Zvyozdochkin created the very first nesting doll in 1890. Often the largest doll has the design of a Russian peasant woman, but the inner dolls can be either male or female, with the smallest often a baby.

А	Б	В	Г	Д	Е
Ё	Ж	З	И	Й	К
Л	М	Н	О	П	Р
С	Т	У	Ф	Х	Ц
Ч	Ш	Щ	Ъ	Ы	Ь
Э	Ю	Я			

Bliny are thin, Russian pancakes. They are made out of buckwheat flour and yeast. They can be dipped in cottage cheese, jam, sour cream, or syrup.

Created in the tenth century, the Russian language is written in characters called the Cyrillic alphabet, named after the Byzantium missionary St. Cyril. Some of the letters are based on Greek or Latin alphabetic characters.

AFRICA

COUNTRIES

The nations that make up the continent of Africa comprise an area covering approximately one-fifth of the land on earth. Some of the world's oldest civilizations are here, including that of the Egyptian and Kushite Empires. Throughout the continent a multitude of languages are spoken, including Arabic, English, French, and Portuguese, as well as a variety of tribal languages, including Bantu and Swahili. There is a wondrous diversity of landscapes here, from the Atlas Mountains in the north, across the great **Sahara Desert**, through rainforests and jungles, down the beautiful Victoria Falls, and farther down into the lush green fields and orchards of the southern tip.

① Named by David Livingstone in honor of Queen Victoria, Victoria Falls is one of the world's largest waterfalls, more than half a mile wide. It is on the Zambezi River and has been called "the smoke that thunders" by many African people who have lived near it.

② Kilimanjaro is the highest mountain on the continent of Africa at 19,340 feet (5,895 meters). The first successful ascent was in 1889. Taking anywhere from four to eight days to summit, the name *Kilimanjaro* means "white mountain," and is also known as *Uhuru* ("freedom").

③ The largest artificial lake or reservoir in the world is Lake Kariba between Zambia and Zimbabwe. It was formed by the Kariba Dam.

④ The world's longest river is the Nile, flowing 4,130 miles through ten countries, from Tanzania all the way to Egypt, finally emptying into the Mediterranean Sea.

⑤ Timbuktu, which became a settlement of the Tuareg Imashagan people in the 12th century, is in the western African nation of Mali on the southern edge of the Sahara Desert. It is noted on the UNESCO World Heritage Site listing as a cultural location for preservation. When someone says, "From here to Timbuktu," now you'll know where!

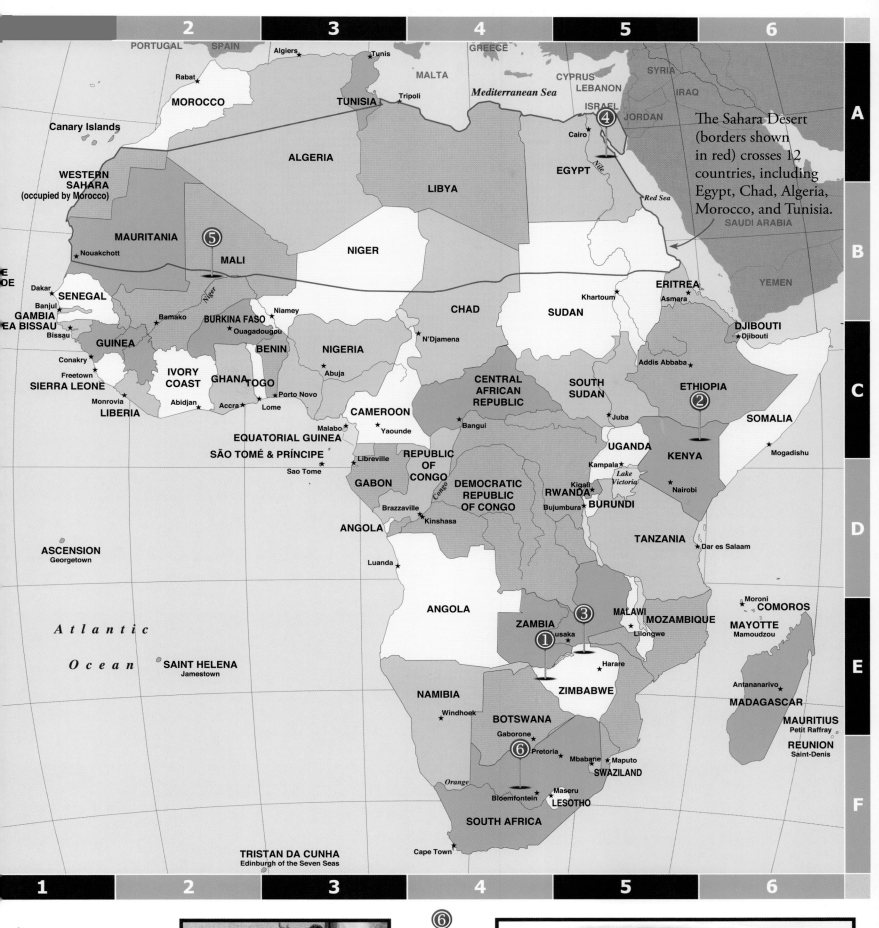

PORTUGAL SPAIN

A
B
C
D
E
F

2 3 4 5 6

Rabat ★

MOROCCO

Algiers ★   ★ Tunis

TUNISIA

Tripoli ★

GREECE

MALTA

Mediterranean Sea

CYPRUS
LEBANON
SYRIA
IRAQ

ISRAEL ④ JORDAN

Cairo ★

EGYPT

Nile

Red Sea

SAUDI ARABIA

The Sahara Desert
(borders shown
in red) crosses 12
countries, including
Egypt, Chad, Algeria,
Morocco, and Tunisia.

Canary Islands

**WESTERN
SAHARA**
(occupied by Morocco)

ALGERIA

LIBYA

MAURITANIA

★ Nouakchott

⑤

MALI

NIGER

Niger

YEMEN

Dakar ★

SENEGAL
Banjul ★
GAMBIA
EA BISSAU Bissau ★

GUINEA

Conakry ★

Freetown ★
SIERRA LEONE
Monrovia ★
LIBERIA

Bamako ★

BURKINA FASO
Niamey ★
★ Ouagadougou

BENIN

**IVORY
COAST**
Abidjan ★
GHANA TOGO
Accra ★ Lome ★
★ Porto Novo

NIGERIA

Abuja ★

CHAD

N'Djamena ★

SUDAN

Khartoum ★

ERITREA
Asmara ★

DJIBOUTI
★ Djibouti

Addis Abbaba ★

ETHIOPIA
②

CAMEROON

Malabo ★
EQUATORIAL GUINEA
SÃO TOMÉ & PRÍNCIPE
Sao Tome ★

Yaounde ★

**CENTRAL
AFRICAN
REPUBLIC**
Bangui ★

**SOUTH
SUDAN**

Juba ★

SOMALIA

★ Mogadishu

Libreville ★
GABON

**REPUBLIC
OF
CONGO**

Congo

**DEMOCRATIC
REPUBLIC
OF CONGO**

UGANDA
Kampala ★
Kigali ★
RWANDA ★
Bujumbura ★
BURUNDI

KENYA
*Lake
Victoria*
Nairobi ★

Brazzaville ★
ANGOLA
Kinshasa ★

TANZANIA

Dar es Salaam ★

ASCENSION
Georgetown

Luanda ★

Moroni ★ **COMOROS**

MAYOTTE
Mamoudzou

Atlantic

Ocean
SAINT HELENA
Jamestown ★

ANGOLA

ZAMBIA
① Lusaka ★
③

MALAWI
Lilongwe ★

MOZAMBIQUE

Harare ★

ZIMBABWE

NAMIBIA

Windhoek ★

BOTSWANA
Gaborone ★
⑥ ★ Pretoria

Antananarivo ★
MADAGASCAR

MAURITIUS
Petit Raffray

REUNION
Saint-Denis

Orange

Mbabane ★ ★ Maputo
SWAZILAND

Maseru ★
Bloemfontein ★ **LESOTHO**

SOUTH AFRICA

TRISTAN DA CUNHA
Edinburgh of the Seven Seas

Cape Town ★

1 2 3 4 5 6

Born in
Scotland, David
Livingstone
(1813–1873) is perhaps
one of the most famous
missionaries of all
time. He was the first
European to explore
the interior of Africa,
wanting to spread the
gospel and find a way
of ending the horrid
slave trade.

⑥

Diamonds
are highly
prized
minerals,
formed deep
in the earth
and brought
closer to
the surface

through volcanic activity. Around half of all diamond production
occurs in African mines, many of which are in South Africa. Historic
Kimberley diamond mine shown above, is a World Heritage Site.

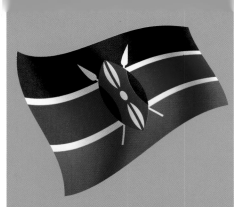

FLAG AND MEANING: There are three equal horizontal bands of black, red, and green; the red band is edged in white; a large Maasai warrior's shield covering crossed spears is superimposed at the center; black symbolizes the majority population; red the blood shed in the struggle for freedom; green stands for natural wealth; and white for peace. The shield and crossed spears symbolize the defense of freedom.

Capital City	Nairobi
Government System	Republic
Primary Languages	English and Kiswahili
Population	43,013,341
Monetary Unit	Kenyan shilling
Area	360,623 sq. miles
National Symbol	Lion
National Anthem	"Ee Mungu Nguvu Yetu" ("Oh God of All Creation")
Largest City	Nairobi 3,375,000

The Republic of Kenya takes its name from **Mount Kenya,** the second-highest mountain in Africa. It actually has peaks that are covered in snow all year. The nation lies on the equator and is on the far eastern portion of Africa, with the **Indian Ocean** on its southeastern border. The weather and landscapes are varied across the country. Near the ocean there is a much warmer, wetter environment. Further inland, there are beautiful savannah grasslands where wildlife thrives. Many people come to these areas in Kenya for the animal safaris. On the western edge of the country one finds hills, forests, and the magnificent Lake Victoria. There are even desert areas that stretch across portions of the land.

① The largest of Africa's lakes is Lake Victoria. It is actually in three countries: Kenya, Tanzania, and Uganda. It is considered the largest tropical lake on earth.

Giant pangolins live where there are many termites and ants, their main food source. Also called scaly anteaters, they have a very good sense of smell and hunt across forests and savannas at night.

BIOME
Grasslands

Grasslands cover about one-fourth of earth's land. They are found where there is too little rain for trees and more rain than a desert receives. In South America they are known as pampas. If you're in the United States they are called prairies. In Russia they are called steppes. And in Africa they are called savannas. Herds of eland, wildebeest, and elephants roam and feed here. Giraffes eat leaves from the few acacia trees that grow where there is enough water. Lions and wild dogs hunt the animals that thrive here, forming a perfect balance.

Africa has a rich history of Christian faith. The Ethiopian eunuch mentioned in Acts chapter 8, who was reading Isaiah, was baptized by Philip. Many believe he carried the faith much deeper into the heart of the continent. Some also credit Catholic Portuguese traders with introducing Christianity to Kenya in the late 15th century.

Dr. Johann Ludwig Krapf founded the first Christian mission in 1846. The Church Missionary Society of England helped send this German explorer and linguist to Mijikenda on the Kenyan coast. Krapf was one of the first Europeans to see Mount Kenya, and he translated the Bible into Swahili.

Freretown in Kenya was established by Christians as a safe haven for freed and escaped slaves from as far away as Malawi, Tanzania, and Zambia. The Kengeleni church was built there in 1875, and many of those who were freed worshiped here.

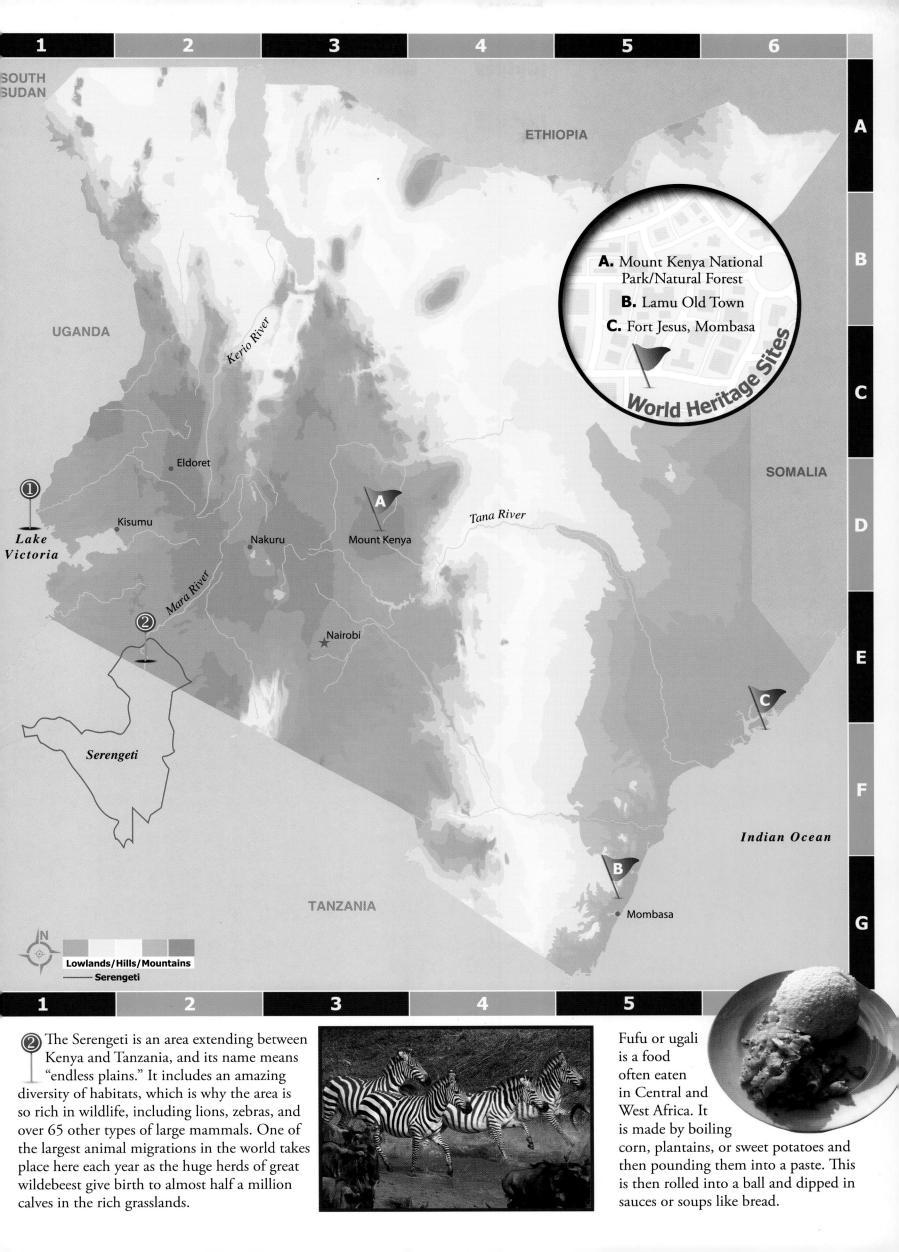

SOUTH SUDAN

ETHIOPIA

A. Mount Kenya National Park/Natural Forest
B. Lamu Old Town
C. Fort Jesus, Mombasa

World Heritage Sites

UGANDA

Kerio River

SOMALIA

Eldoret

① *Lake Victoria*

Kisumu

Nakuru

A

Mount Kenya

Tana River

Mara River

②

Nairobi

C

Serengeti

Indian Ocean

B

TANZANIA

Mombasa

N

Lowlands/Hills/Mountains
Serengeti

② The Serengeti is an area extending between Kenya and Tanzania, and its name means "endless plains." It includes an amazing diversity of habitats, which is why the area is so rich in wildlife, including lions, zebras, and over 65 other types of large mammals. One of the largest animal migrations in the world takes place here each year as the huge herds of great wildebeest give birth to almost half a million calves in the rich grasslands.

Fufu or ugali is a food often eaten in Central and West Africa. It is made by boiling corn, plantains, or sweet potatoes and then pounding them into a paste. This is then rolled into a ball and dipped in sauces or soups like bread.

FLAG AND MEANING: There are three equal horizontal bands of red, white, and black; the national emblem (a gold Eagle of Saladin facing the hoist side with a shield superimposed on its chest above a scroll bearing the name of the country in Arabic) centered in the white band; the band colors derive from the Arab Liberation flag and represent oppression (black), overcome through bloody struggle (red), to be replaced by a bright future (white).

Capital City	Cairo
Government System	Republic
Primary Languages	Arabic
Population	83,688,164
Monetary Unit	Egyptian pound
Area	622,272 sq. miles
National Symbol	Golden eagle
National Anthem	"Bilady, Bilady, Bilady" ("My Homeland, My Homeland, My Homeland")
Largest City	Cairo 10,902,000

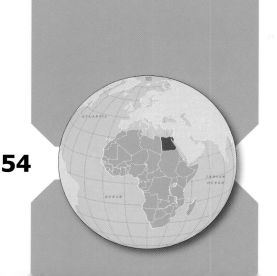

The rich history of Egypt goes back thousands of years, connecting with much of the Bible's history as well. For hundreds of years it was the dominant power in northern Africa and the Middle East. The **Mediterranean Sea** borders the north of the country, with the Jeddah or **Red Sea** on the eastern line. The great **Nile River** flows from the south to the north edge. It is around this river that the majority of the people live because of the fertile soil that the flooding river provides. This is why the ancient name of the country in Egyptian is *Kemet*. It means "black land," as the rich soil is a deep black. Life has thrived on the river since before the time of Christ.

The hottest desert on earth is the Sahara Desert. It is also the third largest in the world. The entire country of Egypt is located within the Sahara. The desert itself is nearly the size of the United States, and some of the sand dunes can be nearly 600 feet high.

Many of the desert-dwelling tribes are called Bedouins. These groups of people live in small family groups that move from place to place, living in tents or structures that can be easily taken down and moved. Camels are used for transportation, meat, and milk. Since the early 1900s, some Bedouin groups have given up this nomadic or mobile lifestyle.

① History here is filled with a sense of mystery. There are the mummies discovered in the Valley of the Kings, the marvelous Sphinx, ancient temples, and the Khufu ship found completely intact inside the Giza pyramid. The Pyramids at Giza are nearly 4,000 years old, and are the only surviving relic of the Seven Wonders of the Ancient World.

Samuel Zwemer (1867–1952) was a missionary who felt a calling to reach Muslims with the gospel message. Working from Cairo, Egypt, he spent much of his life sharing the love of Jesus throughout much of the Islamic world in the Middle East.

Biblical history reveals that Joseph, Mary, and their young child Jesus fled to Egypt to escape Herod's wrath. When Herod died, they returned safely home to Israel. The prophet Hosea referred to this when God said "Out of Egypt I called my son" (Hosea 11:1). The apostle Matthew in the New Testament refers to Jesus fulfilling this prophecy as well.

The majority of Christians in Egypt are called Coptic Christians, a word that translates to "Egyptian." Their history reaches back to the visitation here by Jesus' family and the Early Church of the first century. Saint Mark is said to be the founder of the church as he was martyred in Alexandria in A.D. 68.

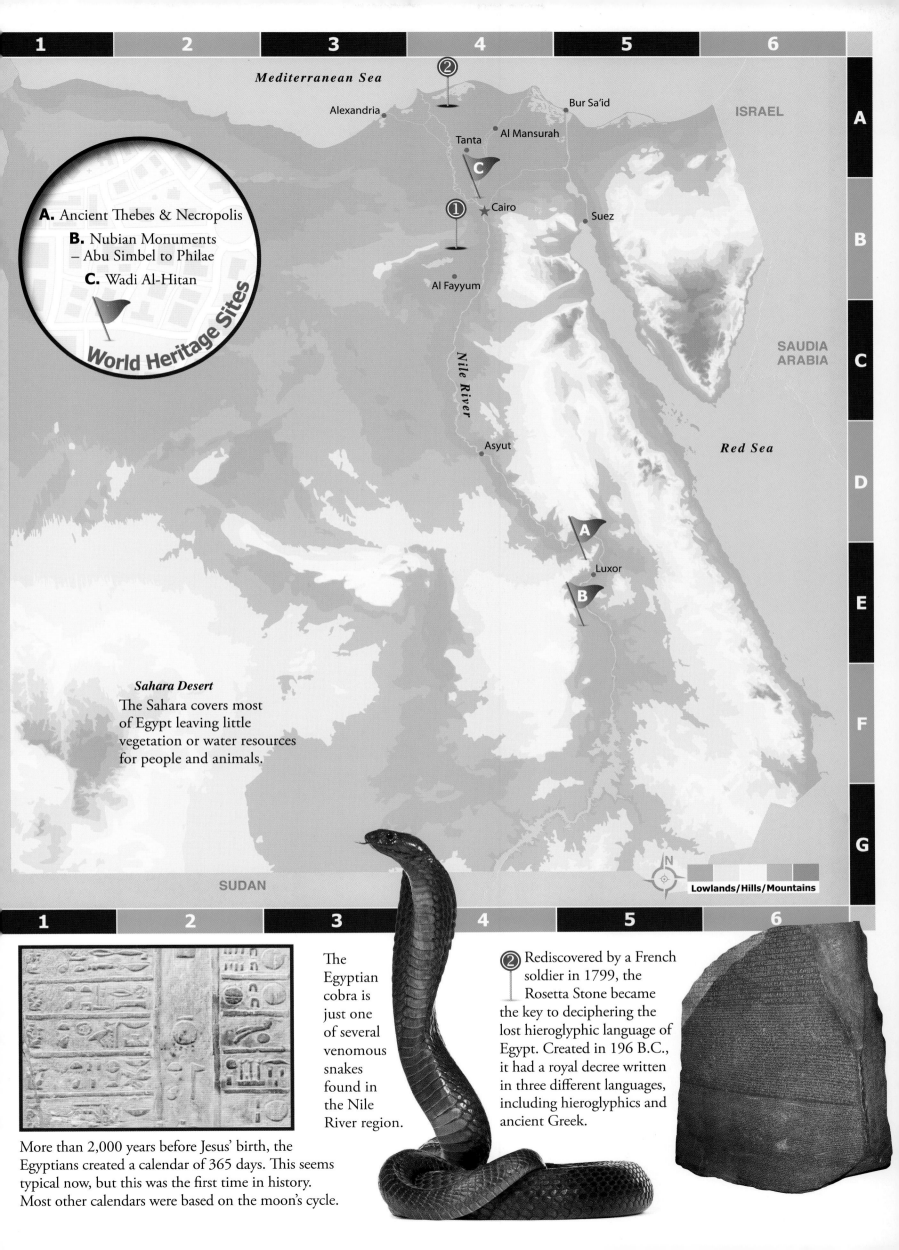

World Heritage Sites

A. Ancient Thebes & Necropolis

B. Nubian Monuments
– Abu Simbel to Philae

C. Wadi Al-Hitan

Mediterranean Sea

Alexandria

Bur Sa'id

ISRAEL

Tanta   Al Mansurah

Cairo

Suez

Al Fayyum

SAUDIA
ARABIA

Nile River

Asyut

Red Sea

A

Luxor

B

Sahara Desert
The Sahara covers most
of Egypt leaving little
vegetation or water resources
for people and animals.

SUDAN

Lowlands/Hills/Mountains

The
Egyptian
cobra is
just one
of several
venomous
snakes
found in
the Nile
River region.

② Rediscovered by a French
soldier in 1799, the
Rosetta Stone became
the key to deciphering the
lost hieroglyphic language of
Egypt. Created in 196 B.C.,
it had a royal decree written
in three different languages,
including hieroglyphics and
ancient Greek.

More than 2,000 years before Jesus' birth, the
Egyptians created a calendar of 365 days. This seems
typical now, but this was the first time in history.
Most other calendars were based on the moon's cycle.

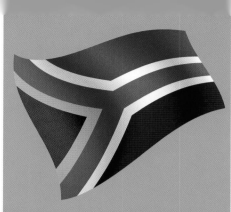

FLAG AND MEANING: There are two equal-width horizontal bands of red and blue separated by a central green band that splits into a horizontal Y, ending at the corners of the left side. The Y embraces a black triangle separated by narrow yellow bands; the red and blue bands are separated from the green band and its arms by narrow white stripes. The colors do not have any official symbolism, but the Y stands for "... taking the road ahead in unity."

Capital City	Pretoria (administrative capital); Cape Town (legislative capital); Bloemfontein (judicial capital)
Government System	Republic
Primary Languages	IsiZulu, IsiXhosa, and Afrikaans
Population	48,810,427
Monetary Unit	South African rand
Area	757,507 sq. miles
National Symbol	Springbok antelope
National Anthem	Lyrics of "Nikosi Sikelel' iAfika" & "Die Stem"
Largest City	Johannesburg 3,607,000

The Republic of South Africa is at the very tip of the African continent. There is a rich cultural history here. It is rooted in the many influences from the native African peoples and the 11 official languages spoken here. Also, there is a Dutch influence, and the Afrikaans language is rooted in that history. It was back in 1652 that the first Dutch traders traveled here. It was to provide a safe place to stop while going back and forth between the Netherlands and the Far East. This safe place became the city of **Cape Town** (above). The 19th-century discovery of diamonds and gold brought many more settlers to the area.

Table Mountain is a plateau overlooking Cape Town that draws many tourists and climbers each year. The first European to make the ascent of the mountain was António de Saldanha in 1503. This Portuguese explorer carved a cross into the Lion's Head rock that is still visible.

Chacma baboons are a major tourist attraction near the Cape of Good Hope. They are considered to be endangered in some areas of South Africa. The loss of habitat and conflicts with people who kill them if they enter cities looking for food are two major reasons for concern.

Robert Moffat became a missionary to South Africa in 1816. Influencing others like David Livingstone to venture into the wilderness of Africa, Moffat's daughter Mary became Livingstone's wife. Moffat translated both the Bible and *The Pilgrim's Progress* into Setswana, a native language in the area.

The Lovedale Mission Station was a missions and educational institution founded in 1824 by the Glasgow Missionary Society in Eastern Cape Province. As an early place of learning, it would allow native boys and girls, as well as Europeans, to attend classes with no racial barriers. It included a primary and high school, a technical school, theological college, hospital, and teacher's college.

John Dugmore's family arrived in South Africa in 1820 after his father lost everything in England after paying a relative's debts. By 1830, Dugmore was involved in a Christian church and studying to be a pastor. During the next 20 years, he became fluent in the Xhosa language, translating the Bible and many hymns that are still sung today. Even after retiring to Queenstown, he continued to influence others.

Lowlands/Hills/Mountains

ZIMBABWE

Limpopo River

BOTSWANA

MOZAMBIQUE

• Polokwane

A

Mmabatho
•   Pretoria ★   • Nelspruit
B   Johannesburg •
Soweto •   SWAZILAND

NAMIBIA

C
Orange River

Kimberley •

Bloemfontein ★

LESOTHO

Pietermaritzburg
•
Durban •

*South
Atlantic
Ocean*

*Indian
Ocean*

①
② Cape Town
     ★

Bisho •

③

Port Elizabeth •

Southern Ocean

② Cape of Good Hope was once thought to be the southern tip of Africa, an important waypoint to sailors trying to sail around the continent to lands in the Far East. It was also a city where people came to escape religious persecution like Huguenots did in the 17th and 18th centuries, and to find opportunities for land and possible wealth.

③ The actual southern tip of the continent is Cape Agulhas. The area was feared by sailers because of fierce winter storms and massive waves.

A. iSimangaliso Wetland Park

B. Vredefort Dome

C. Richtersveld Cultural and Botanical Landscape

World Heritage Sites

Samosas or samoosas are a popular food served here. They are basically fried pancakes stuffed with meat or vegetables or both! They can also be baked if one prefers this healthier method. Samosas are believed to have originated in the Middle East.

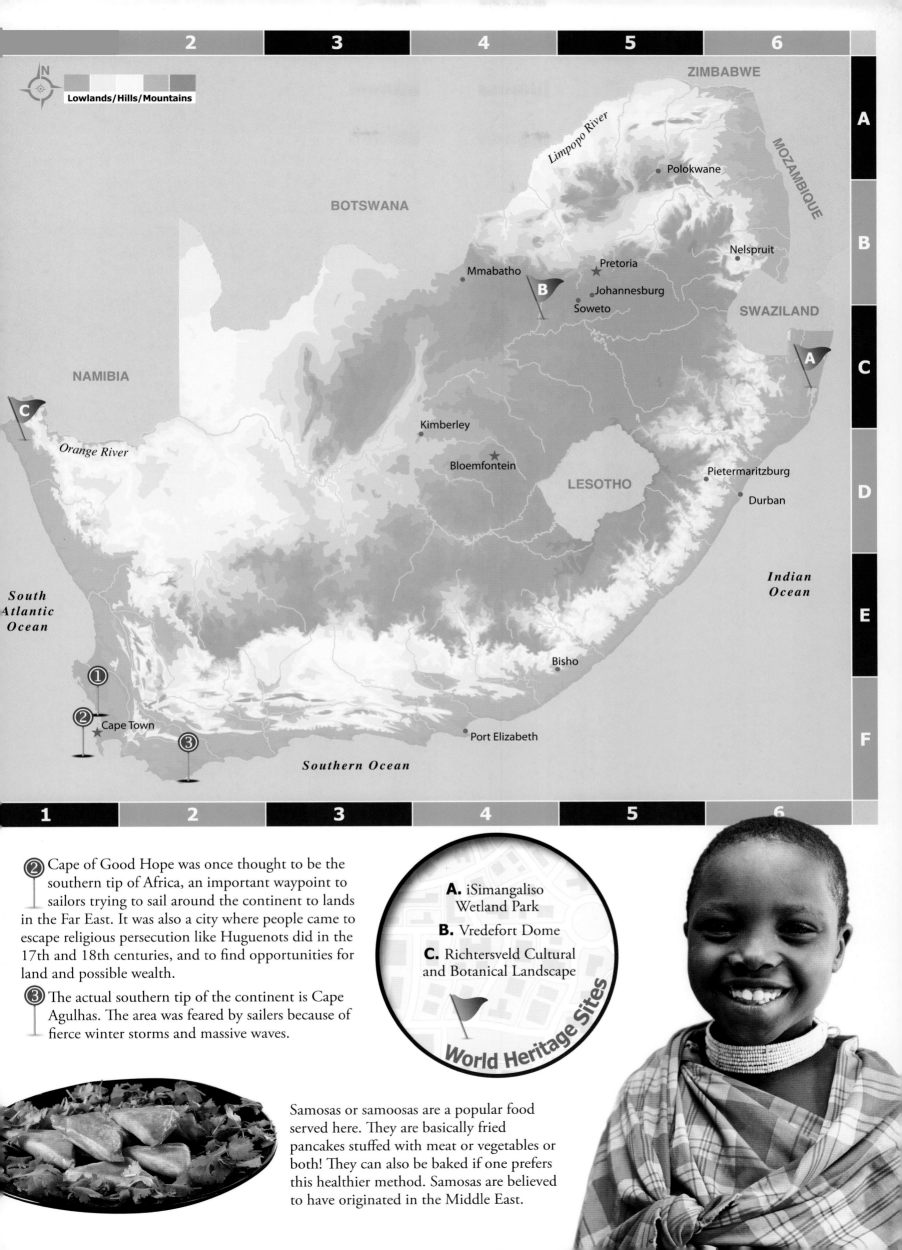

ASIA

Asia is by far the largest continent at nearly 17 million square miles. With over 4 billion people, Asia is home to more than half of the earth's population. Mount Everest, the highest mountain on earth, is here, as is the lowest place on land, the Dead Sea that actually lies below sea level. Several countries, including **Kazakhstan**, **Kyrgyzstan**, and **Tajikistan** were once part of the former Soviet Union (now **Russia**).

1 The area of Asia called the Middle East has been the birthplace of many great ancient civilizations, including the Assyrian, Babylonian, and Persian empires. Here one can find the Tigris and Euphrates rivers. Most of the people here speak Arabic, though in Iran the primary language is Farsi. Within the small country called Israel, God chose to send His Son Jesus to redeem the world. Here, many people still speak Hebrew, the main language of the Old Testament.

2 Mount Everest in Nepal is 29,035 feet (8,848 meters) high, making it the highest mountain on earth. The first successful ascent was in 1953. Everest, also known as *Sagarmāthā* ("holy mother"), normally takes seven to ten weeks to summit. Nepal's flag is the only country flag that is not in the shape of a rectangle or square. Sherpas are originally from Tibet, and often help climbers summit Everest. They can carry excessively heavy loads and survive extreme climates. *Sher* is a word that means "east" and *pa* is a word that means "people."

3 Built perhaps as early as 300 years before the birth of Christ, Petra is a remarkable stone city. And the very name means "stone" or "rock." Carved from stone over hundreds of years, it was first the capital city of a people known as the Nabataeans. Lying hidden within the surrounding stone mountains, it was not discovered by those outside this land until 1812. A Swiss explorer by the name of Johann Ludwig Burckhardt looked on it in wonder and reported back to the Western world about its beauty.

4 Not only is Istanbul, Turkey, considered one of the most beautiful, exotic cities in the world, it's also one of the few on two continents! This seaport city and ancient former capital of the Byzantine and Ottoman Empires actually rests in both Europe and Asia! The other three transcontinental cities are Atyrau in Kazakhstan and Orenburg in Russia, both in Europe and Asia, and Suez in Egypt that is in both Africa and Asia.

GREENLAND

ICELAND

Arctic Circle

Greenland Sea

Norwegian Sea

North Sea

NORWAY

SWEDEN

FINLAND

Baltic Sea

Barents Sea

Kara Sea

Leptev Sea

Chukchi Sea

Bering Sea

Arctic Ocean

A

B

Pacific Ocean

ESTONIA
LATVIA
LITHUANIA

BYLARUS

Moscow

R U S S I A

Ob'

Yenisey

Volga

UKRAINE
ROMANIA
MOLDOVA
BULGARIA

④

Angara

Lena

Lena

Aldan

Amur

Sea of Okhotsk

Sea of Japan
(East Sea)

Black Sea

Ank

①

③

TURKEY

GEORGIA
ARMENIA
AZERBAIJAN

Caspian Sea

Astana

KAZAKHSTAN

Irtish

Ulaanbaatar

MONGOLIA

Beijing

NORTH
KOREA

Pyongyang

Seoul

SOUTH
KOREA

Tokyo

JAPAN

C

LEBANON
SYRIA

RAEL
JORDAN

IRAQ

Baghdad

Tehran

Aral Sea

UZBEKISTAN

TURKMENISTAN

Ashgabat

Tashkent

Bishkek

KYRGYZSTAN

Dushanbe

TAJIKISTAN

L. Balkhash

Hwang

Yellow Sea

East China Sea

Tropic of Cancer

KUWAIT

Riyadh

BAHRAIN
QATAR

U. A. E.

IRAN

AFGHANISTAN

Kabul

Islamabad

PAKISTAN

②

C H I N A

Yangtze

TAIWAN

D

SAUDI ARABIA

Muscat

Sanaa

YEMEN

OMAN

Arabian Sea

New Delhi

India

NEPAL

Kathmandu

BHUTAN

Ganges

BANGLADESH

Dhaka

Hanoi

South China Sea

Manila

PHILIPPINES

OMALIA

Indian Ocean

INDIA

MYANMAR

Rangoon

Bay of Bengal

Salween

LAOS

Vientiane

THAILAND

Mekong

VIETNAM

E

SRI LANKA

Colombo

Bangkok

CAMBODIA

Phnom Penh

BRUNEI

Equator

MALAYSIA

Kuala Lumpur

SINGAPORE

MALAYSIA

I N D O N E S I A

Dili

EAST TIMOR

AUSTRALIA

F

Jakarta

Sloth bears are rather noisy as they dig and grunt in search of food at night. In their hunts, they love to devour beetles, grubs, termites, and other insects, as well as fruit. In the Hindi language the word for bear is *bhalu*. This word was the inspiration for the name of the bear in Rudyard Kipling's *The Jungle Book*.

Camel spiders live in the shadows of the desert, and the combined length of the head and body can be up to six inches in length! They are not poisonous, but their bite can sometimes poke through skin. These spiders can run up to 10 miles per hour, though they rarely attack.

FLAG AND MEANING: It is white with a blue hexagram (six-pointed star) known as the Magen David (Shield of David) centered between two equal horizontal blue bands near the top and bottom edges of the flag. The basic design resembles a Jewish prayer shawl (*tallit*), which is white with blue stripes; the hexagram as a Jewish symbol dates back to medieval times.

Capital City	Jerusalem
Government System	Parliamentary democracy
Primary Languages	Hebrew, Arabic, and English
Population	7,590,758
Monetary Unit	New Israeli shekel
Area	12,905 sq. miles
National Symbol	Star of David
National Anthem	"Hatikvah" ("The Hope")
Largest City	Jerusalem 780,200

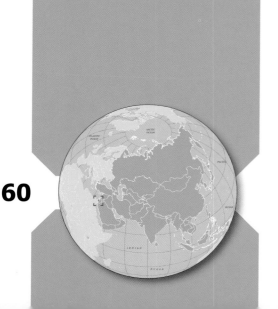

On the far eastern shore of the **Mediterranean Sea** is the country of Israel. Though considered small in size, it has had perhaps the greatest influence worldwide. Historically, it has been a land of conflict, invasion, and war for thousands of years. The nation of Israel began at the time God called Abram (Abraham) from his homeland to this Promised Land. Israel was at the crossroads of ancient civilization, being close to such powerful kingdoms as Egypt, Mesopotamia, and the Roman Empire. The people of Israel were scattered not long after the birth of the church, but God gathered them again, and the land of Israel once more became a country on May 14, 1948.

① The Dead Sea or Salt Sea is the earth's lowest elevation on land. It is actually over 1,300 feet below sea level! This sea is essentially a salt lake, and one of the saltiest bodies of water in the world. There is more than eight times as much salt in the water as there is in the ocean. The caves of Khirbet Qumran nearby are where two boys stumbled upon what have come to be called the Dead Sea Scrolls. These scrolls contain biblical passages from 100 years before Jesus' birth.

② The town of Bethlehem is located in the controversial West Bank, under the control of the Palestinian Authority, which also oversees the Gaza Strip. A large percentage of Palestinian Christians live in the city, which is also visited by tourists. As has happened for centuries, Israel and this area of the world known as the Holy Land remain a site of controversy. Peace has been difficult to find as Israel finds itself surrounded by countries that actively and politically seek its destruction.

The Torah is the first portion of the Hebrew Bible, which is called the *Tanakh*. The name *Torah* means "instruction" or "teaching." These are also the first five books of the Bible: Genesis, Exodus, Leviticus, Numbers, and Deuteronomy, and were given by God to Moses. They lay a vital foundation for both Judaism and Christianity.

Jesus was born in Bethlehem, lived in the city of Nazareth, walked upon the Sea of Galilee (above), was crucified outside Jerusalem on a hill called Golgatha ("the place of the skull"), and three days later rose again to bring salvation to the world.

Jerusalem, one of the oldest cities in the world, has been given the name City of Peace. It has strong spiritual significance for Jews, as well as Christians and Muslims. It is here that Jesus walked and shared of His life and God's divine purposes, and it is here He was crucified and three days later rose from the dead.

③ The Western Wall or Wailing Wall is one of the remaining ruins of the Second Temple in Old Jerusalem. It is a holy site for Jews around the world who often travel to pray at the site. Jewish law requires men to have their head covered while praying. Often kippahs or yarmulkes, which are small round hats, are worn. Visitors can also see members of the Hasidic Jewish community praying here. The community is distinctive in their clothing — men wear long, dark coats, dark hats, and dark shoes. Many Jewish people place prayers within the stones of the Wailing Wall. This is the only portion that remains from the temple of Jesus' day. The temple was almost completely destroyed by the Romans in A.D. 70.

A. Biblical Tels (Megiddo, Hazor, Beer Sheba)
B. Incense Route
C. Old City of Acre

World Heritage Sites

Lowlands/Hills/Mountains
------- Disputed territory

④ While many think of Israel in terms of ancient biblical times, the nation is also a modern thriving one. Tel Aviv, the second-largest city in Israel, is filled with skyscrapers and serves as an economic center. Israel claims Jerusalem as its capital city, but the international community has not yet recognized it as such. Therefore most foreign embassies are in Tel Aviv.

The shofar is a horn, traditionally that of a ram, used for Jewish religious purposes, and sometimes used in Christian churches as well. Sounding the shofar is part of synagogue services on the holy days of Rosh Hashanah and Yom Kippur. A synagogue is the place of worship for those of the Jewish faith. People of Jewish heritage who recognize Christ as their Messiah are known as Messianic Jews. They call Jesus *Yeshua*, which is the Hebrew name for "Joshua" and would have been how Jesus' name was pronounced. They see the Old Testament fulfilled in the life of Christ, and many thousands live in Israel.

Between the months of February and March is the Jewish month called *Adar*. During this month the festival of Purim is celebrated. It is a vibrant celebration of the historic account of Esther from the Bible. It was the Jewish Queen Esther who saved her people from their planned slaughter by Haman, an evil counselor to her husband, the Persian king. During this festival there is an exchange of gifts, called *Mishloach Manot*, plays to re-enact the account, and wonderful foods. *Hamantashen* are pastries that are shaped like triangles, and *Purim challah* is a woven bread loaf sprinkled with icing or poppy seeds.

More than half of Israel's land is desert, with little to no useful water supplies. However, they are also known for their agricultural expertise and technology. They actually provide all but five percent of the total food needed for the nation. Israel is able to export much fresh produce.

The hoopoe is Israel's national bird. It thrives in areas with little to no vegetation where it searches to find insects, seeds, and berries. It seeks openings within vertical spaces or cliffs where it can nest. It loves to sunbathe and take dust baths.

Jewish *burekas* are pastries stuffed with assorted fillings, including feta cheese, spinach, or other vegetables. They are then baked or fried. One can use strudel dough or phyllo dough, and they are best served hot and fresh.

⑤ The Hall of Names at Yad Vashem is a tragic reminder of the devastation brought on the Jewish people of Europe during the Nazi control of Germany before and during World War II. With millions being murdered and millions more forced to work in concentration camps, these events are called the Holocaust, and it remains one of the darkest periods of modern history. Yad Vashem, located on the Mount of Remembrance, was established in 1953 as the country's official memorial to the millions of Jewish victims. The museum helps to educate others about the horrors of the Holocaust and honor the lives of those lost.

Kibbutz is a Hebrew word that means "community settlement." In Israel this is a group of people who live and work together in a rural setting and share certain values of social justice, cooperation, and education. They come together to help provide everything they can to assist the needs of those in their extended "family" group. Many are agricultural sites that are designed to preserve water and develop seeds like special sunflowers that are disease resistant.

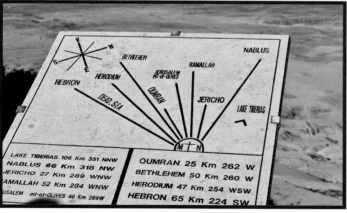

⑥ The mountaintop fortress of Masada (right) represents an important event in the history of Israel. During Roman repression of the Jewish people and destruction of the Second Temple in A.D. 70, a determined group of 960 took refuge at Masada. Roman soldiers laid siege to it and worked to build a ramp to gain entrance. After months of refusing to surrender, as the Romans began breaking through the walls, the 960 Jews set fire to the fort and chose death rather than slavery to Rome. From Masada you can see many of the key biblical cities, demonstrating how tiny the nation of Israel truly is.

FLAG AND MEANING:

Green is a traditional color in Islamic flags. The *Shahada* or Muslim creed in large white Arabic script (translated as "There is no god but God; Muhammad is the Messenger of God") is above a white horizontal saber. The design dates to the early 20th century and is associated with the Al Saud family, which established the kingdom in 1932.

Capital City	Riyadh
Government System	Monarchy
Primary Languages	Arabic
Population	26,534,504
Monetary Unit	Saudi riyal
Area	1,335,755 sq. miles
National Symbol	Palm tree surmounting two crossed swords
National Anthem	"Aash Al Maleek" ("Long Live Our Beloved King")
Largest City	Riyadh 5,328,228

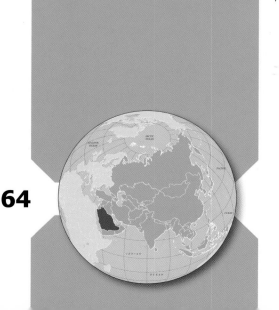

Bordering the **Red Sea**, the history of the land and people in the region now known as Saudi Arabia is rich and varied. Ancient records show their influence with such cultures as Babylon, Egypt, Greece, and Persia. The great desert portions of the terrain helped protect the people from invasion. With Arabic as its language, the area developed a long era of scientific advances. This came to be known as the "Golden Age." Many Muslim scholars of this time made advancements in astronomy, biology, literature, and medicine. In 1932, the current kingdom was established by Abdul-Aziz bin Saud. It is considered an Islamic state with the Quran (Koran) as its constitution. Much of the wealth of the nation comes from oil. Saudi Arabia has roughly one-fifth of the world's known oil reserves.

① The city of Mecca is considered the holiest city of Islam. It is here that the prophet Mohammed was born. The religion of Islam came from his writings, called the Quran (Koran). During the course of a day, Muslims around the world bow in prayer five times in the direction of Mecca. This is at dawn, at noon, in the afternoon, the evening, and one final time at night. Millions come to the city in what is called the *hajj*, a pilgrimage that all Muslims who have the means are asked to do.

Saudi Arabia has three major deserts, which cover half of the country. **Ad Dahna** is a narrow desert of red sand in the central portion of the country. It actually links all three major deserts. **An Nafud** is a red sand, upland desert. Horrible sandstorms are driven by fierce winds that shape mammoth sand dunes. The **Rub' al Khali** is one of the largest sand deserts on the earth, and it stretches to the surrounding countries of Oman, the United Arab Emirates, and Yemen. The vast Arabian Desert is made up of these three smaller desert lands and extends across a large part of this region of the world. Even in this barren place there are gazelles, oryx, sand cats, and other creatures that thrive.

Arabic calligraphy is the beautiful writing style of the region that originated in the 6th century. It is written from right to left and is the language of the Quran. Writing in Ottoman calligraphy from the 18th century depicts the phrase "In the name of God, Most Merciful, Most Gracious."

One of the first church buildings ever constructed has been found here by archaeologists. Built around the 4th century, it has come to be called the Jubail Church. Many congregations of Christians once thrived here until they were killed or driven out by the growth of Islam at the end of the first millennium.

No religion other than Islam is allowed to be practiced in Saudi Arabia. If someone is converted to Christianity, it is considered a crime, and often punishable by death. Because of this harsh view, the official records state that the number of those who claim to be Christians within the country is zero.

Though there are no official churches in the country, those who have faith in Christ do meet. However, other than meeting in public places, these meeting are kept secret or done through the Internet. If foreign Christians enter Saudi Arabia, they are allowed by the government to meet if they officially register.

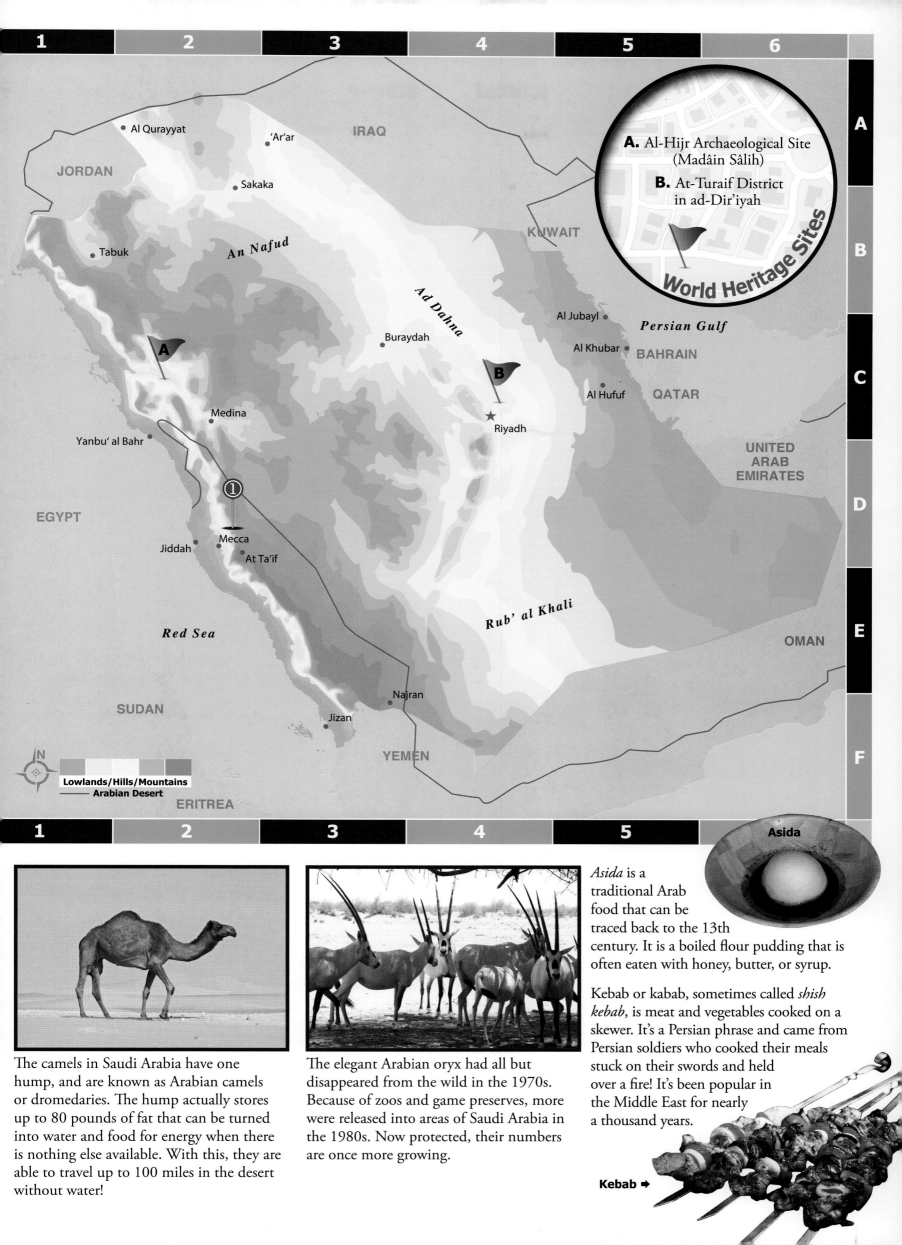

| 1 | 2 | 3 | 4 | 5 | 6 |

IRAQ

- Al Qurayyat
- 'Ar'ar
- Sakaka

JORDAN

World Heritage Sites

A. Al-Hijr Archaeological Site (Madâin Sâlih)

B. At-Turaif District in ad-Dir'iyah

KUWAIT

An Nafud

- Tabuk

Ad Dahna

- Buraydah

Al Jubayl
Persian Gulf

Al Khubar
BAHRAIN

A

B

Al Hufuf
QATAR

- Medina

★ Riyadh

- Yanbu' al Bahr

UNITED ARAB EMIRATES

EGYPT

①

- Mecca
- Jiddah
- At Ta'if

Red Sea

Rub' al Khali

OMAN

SUDAN

- Najran
- Jizan

YEMEN

ERITREA

N

Lowlands/Hills/Mountains
Arabian Desert

| A | B | C | D | E | F |

| 1 | 2 | 3 | 4 | 5 |

Asida

Asida is a traditional Arab food that can be traced back to the 13th century. It is a boiled flour pudding that is often eaten with honey, butter, or syrup.

Kebab or kabab, sometimes called *shish kebab*, is meat and vegetables cooked on a skewer. It's a Persian phrase and came from Persian soldiers who cooked their meals stuck on their swords and held over a fire! It's been popular in the Middle East for nearly a thousand years.

The camels in Saudi Arabia have one hump, and are known as Arabian camels or dromedaries. The hump actually stores up to 80 pounds of fat that can be turned into water and food for energy when there is nothing else available. With this, they are able to travel up to 100 miles in the desert without water!

The elegant Arabian oryx had all but disappeared from the wild in the 1970s. Because of zoos and game preserves, more were released into areas of Saudi Arabia in the 1980s. Now protected, their numbers are once more growing.

Kebab ➡

Capital City	New Delhi
Government System	Federal republic
Primary Languages	Hindi, Bengali, and Telugu
Population	1,205,073,612
Monetary Unit	Indian rupee
Area	2,042,610 sq. miles
National Symbol	Bengal tiger
National Anthem	"Jana-Gana-Mana" ("Thou Art the Ruler of the Minds of All People")
Largest City	Mumbai 12,478,447

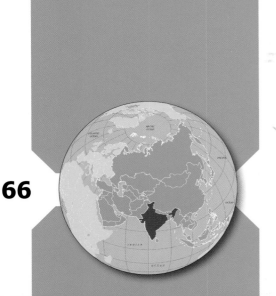

The Republic of India is the second most populated country in the world and the largest democracy, with over one billion people. It has had a long and wondrous history, being at the crossroads of trade routes. Here rose the riches of the Indus Valley civilization, and the four religions of Buddhism, Hinduism, Jainism, and Sikhism. After a long period of British rule, India became an independent nation in 1947, led by Mahatma Gandhi, who was born in **Porbander**. His desire was to fight against the ruling government with non-violent means alone, and his life has inspired others in the fight for freedom and the civil rights of all people.

① The longest river in India is the Ganges or Ganga, which is just over 1,500 miles long. The river ends in the Bay of Bengal, and hundreds of millions of people live along its shores. It is considered a sacred river by the Hindu people.

② The Taj Mahal is a magnificent building of Muslim art constructed in the city of Agra, India. After the untimely death of his wife, the grieving Mughal emperor Shah Jahan had the monument built as a memorial for her. It was started in 1632 and took over 20 years to finish. There is a reflecting pool that extends from the front into the gardens surrounding the memorial.

It was in India that the process of converting sugar cane into crystallized sugar was developed.

Mother Teresa of Calcutta (above) came to serve the poor and oppressed in India. She started a worldwide ministry called the Missionaries of Charity. Those who serve vow to give wholehearted service to the "poorest of the poor." She gave all of her life to provide food and shelter and love for those in need.

Born in Northampton, England, William Carey (1761–1834) is known by many as the father of modern missions, helping complete translations of the Bible into Bengali, Marathi, and Sanskrit. In India, he fought against the practices of widow burning and infanticide, and laid a foundation for justice in modern India.

Starting with a one-year mission in 1954, Mark and Huldah Buntain left for Calcutta. When they saw the suffering of the poor, they began to build up ministries to provide food for the hungry and to teach them about God's love for us all. They built at least 100 schools to minister to children, as well as a hospital.

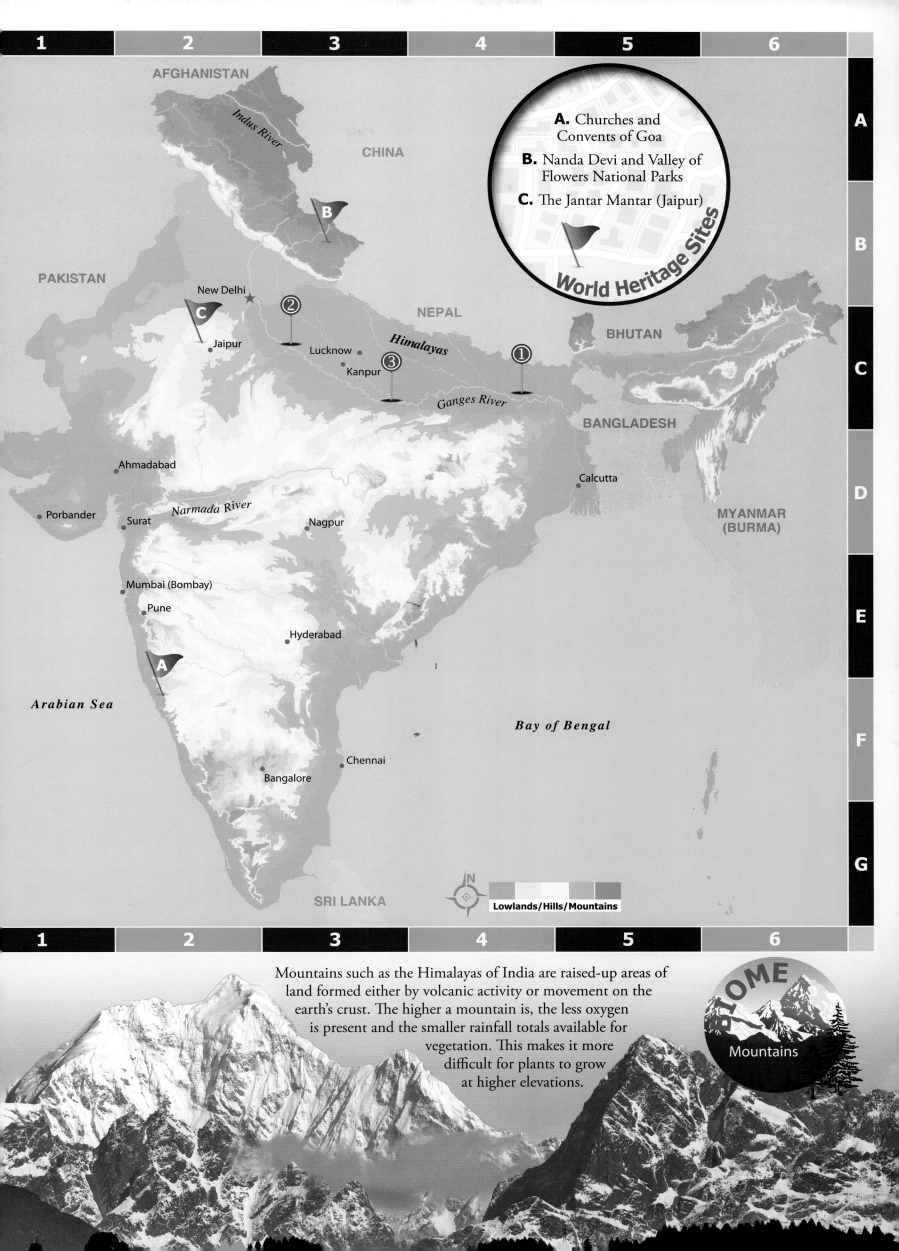

	1	2	3	4	5	6

AFGHANISTAN

Indus River

CHINA

B

PAKISTAN

New Delhi ★

C

Jaipur

②

Lucknow ·

③ Kanpur

Himalayas

NEPAL

①

Ganges River

BHUTAN

BANGLADESH

Ahmadabad ·

Calcutta ·

MYANMAR
(BURMA)

· Porbander

Surat ·

Narmada River

Nagpur ·

Mumbai (Bombay) ·

Pune ·

Hyderabad ·

A

Arabian Sea

Bay of Bengal

Chennai ·

Bangalore ·

SRI LANKA

N

Lowlands/Hills/Mountains

A. Churches and
Convents of Goa

B. Nanda Devi and Valley of
Flowers National Parks

C. The Jantar Mantar (Jaipur)

World Heritage Sites

Mountains such as the Himalayas of India are raised-up areas of
land formed either by volcanic activity or movement on the
earth's crust. The higher a mountain is, the less oxygen
is present and the smaller rainfall totals available for
vegetation. This makes it more
difficult for plants to grow
at higher elevations.

BIOME

Mountains

Many amazing contributions came from India, including the game of chess and the concept of zero, as well as algebra, calculus, and trigonometry.

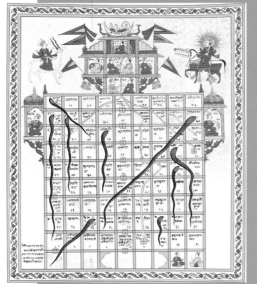

The U.S. board game called Chutes and Ladders has its roots in a game from ancient India that was called *Mokshapat* or *Moksha Patamu*. The ancient game is at least a thousand years old, and was one that taught children moral principles. There were squares with ladders that stood for virtues, as well as those that had snake heads that stood for evil things. Later, the Hindu game was brought to England and the name changed to Snakes and Ladders. There it was eventually changed to just a game of fun without any religious references.

India produces more full-length movies than any other country in the world, with **Bombay** often called Bollywood. People in India attend the movies around three billion times per year!

Chana is a spice-filled Indian meal. The word means "chickpea" in the Hindi language. Along with the chickpeas (also called garbanzo beans), other ingredients are added in, which can include cumin, curry powder, coriander, paprika, tomatoes, and ginger.

English is the most important language for national, political, and commercial communication. Hindi is the most widely spoken language and primary tongue of 41 percent of the people. There are 14 other official languages: Bengali, Telugu, Marathi, Tamil, Urdu, Gujarati, Malayalam, Kannada, Oriya, Punjabi, Assamese, Kashmiri, Sindhi, and Sanskrit.

In August the Hindu festival of *Raksha Bandhan* is celebrated. The name means "bond of protection," and is symbolized by sisters placing woven bracelets called *rakhi* on the wrists of their brothers. The sister prays for her brother to be safe, and he vows to protect her. Special Indian treats are eaten as well, like *barfi*, *gulab*, and *laddu*. This special tradition dates back some 500 years to times of battle.

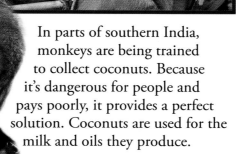

In parts of southern India, monkeys are being trained to collect coconuts. Because it's dangerous for people and pays poorly, it provides a perfect solution. Coconuts are used for the milk and oils they produce.

One of the rarest predators in the world is the snow leopard that lives in the mountainous regions of India. It is medium-sized, compared to lions, tigers, or other larger cats, and can survive quite well in the bitter cold environment.

③ India's history has been impacted by the various empires of which these lands have been a part, including the Mughal Empire. This empire covered much of the subcontinent of Asia in the 1500s to 1700s. The abandoned city of Fatehpur Sikri is a beautiful example of Mughal architecture and planning. Originally named for victory, it was built and served as a new capital of the empire from 1571 to 1585. The city was abandoned after only 15 years due to lack of water and its location being so near areas of increasing turmoil.

Technology and industry are thriving in India. Their telecommunications and automotive industries are some of the fastest growing in the world. Though there is much poverty here, there is a great hope that the people will begin to prosper with this growing economy.

India continues to struggle with issues of water supply and cleaner ways of living, especially in rural areas and poor areas of cities known as slums. The United Nations estimates over 600 million people in the country do not have modern toilets for human waste. Even the largest of cities sometimes provide water just a few hours a day. A huge percentage of wastewater is not treated, ending up in rivers and even the groundwater. An inability to have access to a clean water supply means some use unclean or contaminated water, especially the poor. Visitors to the country routinely develop diarrhea, caused by unsafe water that unfortunately kills hundreds of thousands of Indians each year.

There have long been divisions in Indian society known as the caste system, a form of segregating or separating people based on ethnicity, religion, economic status, or other factors. It can determine what work they do, whom they marry, access to education, and political power. For example, though dance is seen throughout the country for religious festivals and seasonal events, some higher castes discourage dancing as a profession.

Here you see an example of Bharata Natyam, a classical form of dance in which *mudras* or hand gestures retell mythical events. This dancer wears a traditional dress for young girls in southern India called the *pattu pavadai*. It is usually made of silk with a golden border on the bottom.

Cashmere wool, muslin, cotton, calico, buttons, and natural dyes like indigo were long in use in India. Trade helped spread these discoveries and fabrics around the world.

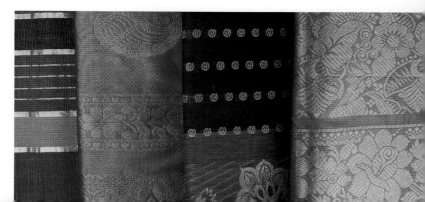

FLAG AND MEANING: It is red with a large, yellow, five-pointed star and four smaller, yellow, five-pointed stars. The color red represents revolution, while the stars symbolize the four social classes — the working class, the peasantry, the urban petty bourgeoisie, and the national bourgeoisie (capitalists) united under the Communist Party of China.

Capital City	Beijing
Government System	Communist state
Primary Languages	Mandarin and Cantonese
Population	1,343,239,923
Monetary Unit	Renminbi
Area	5,963,275 sq. miles
National Symbol	Dragon
National Anthem	"Yiyongjun Jinxingqu" ("The March of the Volunteers")
Largest City	Chongqing 28,846,170

The People's Republic of China has the largest population of any country. The nation is governed by the Communist Party of China. Though there are other existing political parties, including the China Democratic League and the Chinese Peasants' and Workers' Democratic Party, the Communist Party has no real competition for leadership. They rule the 22 provinces, five autonomous regions, and other districts that make up the nation. These include many diverse biomes like subtropical forests, the Gobi desert, the mountain range of the **Himalayas**, vast plateaus, and 9,000 miles of coastline. The country includes the controversial land of **Tibet**, which China took over in 1959 by military action and abolished the government.

The giant panda is a bear that symbolizes China. It has beautiful markings of black and white, and a rounded body. Though they do rarely eat meat, they mostly eat bamboo for food in the wild.

① The longest man-made waterway in the world is the Grand Canal, which extends over 1,000 miles from Bejing to Hangzhou. It has been in use since A.D. 607, and was created to carry grains and rice to the armies and major cities in Northern China. See blue line on map. —

② In 1974 the tomb of China's first emperor, Qin Shihuangdi, who died in 210 B.C. was discovered. Filled with treasures, it was the discovery of his Terra-cotta Army that amazed the world. Almost 8,000 figures have been discovered with detailed uniforms and distinct features. Terra-cotta is a clay-based form of pottery and often used to make flower pots.

A stone tablet from the 8th century, the Nestorian Stele, states that Christians entered the capital of the Tang dynasty in A.D. 635. Christians were given permission to set up places of worship and to make disciples. The leader of the Christians was named Alopen, a Syriac-speaking Persian.

Hudson Taylor (1832–1905), a renowned missionary to China, adopted many Chinese customs to connect the message of the gospel to the people. He inspired many missionaries and evangelists, including Amy Carmichael, Eric Liddell, Jim Elliot, and Billy Graham.

Eric Liddell (1902–1945) was a Christian athlete whose story was made into the movie *Chariots of Fire*. He served as a missionary to China, and died in an internment camp during World War II. Refusing to leave, he gave up his release to a pregnant woman.

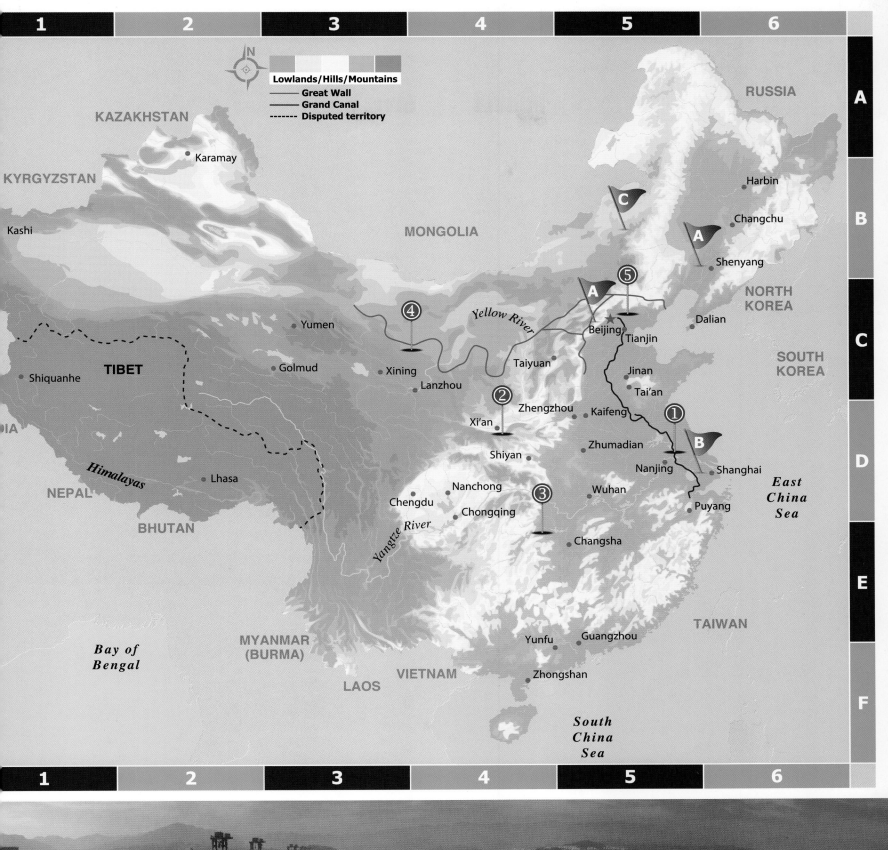

	1	2	3	4	5	6

Lowlands/Hills/Mountains
— Great Wall
— Grand Canal
---- Disputed territory

KAZAKHSTAN

KYRGYZSTAN

Karamay

Kashi

RUSSIA

Harbin

Changchu

C

A

Shenyang

MONGOLIA

NORTH KOREA

SOUTH KOREA

Dalian

Yellow River

④

A

⑤

Beijing

Tianjin

Yumen

TIBET

Shiquanhe

Golmud

Xining

Lanzhou

Taiyuan

Jinan

Tai'an

②

Zhengzhou

Kaifeng

①

Xi'an

Shiyan

Zhumadian

B

Shanghai

Nanjing

Puyang

East China Sea

Himalayas

NEPAL

Lhasa

Chengdu

Nanchong

Chongqing

Yangtze River

③

Wuhan

BHUTAN

IA

Changsha

Bay of Bengal

MYANMAR (BURMA)

Yunfu

Guangzhou

TAIWAN

VIETNAM

LAOS

Zhongshan

South China Sea

	1	2	3	4	5	6

A. Imperial Palaces of the Ming and Qing Dynasties in Beijing and Shenyang

B. Classical Gardens of Suzhou

C. Site of Xanadu

World Heritage Sites

③ The Three Gorges Dam on the Yangtze River was completed in 2012. Over a million people had to be relocated for its construction. Many opposed the project for various reasons, including potential damage to the land and the habitats of many animals. The Chinese government supported the project due to the benefits of huge electric production, increased shipping, and flood control.

Rice is an important crop for China. It is often eaten at every meal, and the farmers here help produce over 25 percent of the world's rice crop.

Translation: Abundant Harvest Year After Year

Written Chinese does not include an alphabet. It has what are called characters, as many as 4,000. They can refer to objects, concepts, or the actual pronunciation of a word. The characters used can represent a whole word, part of a word, or a syllable of a spoken word. Some are also used in written Japanese or Korean.

Paper, much the same as we use today, was first made 2,000 years ago. A man of the royal court of China named Tsai Lun took a mixture of wood pulp and cloth fibers with water, pressed it together and dried it in the sun. It is said that the idea came to him while watching a wasp making its nest. The technology came to the Middle East in the 8th century and Europe in the 14th century. They were using paper money in China as far back as the 7th century. It was another thousand years before paper money was used in Europe!

If you visit a street vendor in Beijing, China, you might find a few exotic foods on the menu. These can include seahorses, cicadas, starfish, and even scorpions! The people of China were eating ice cream thousands of years ago. It was a mixture of snow, milk, and cooked rice.

China invented many items in ancient times that are still used today, including the compass, gun powder, and tea. Tea has been a staple drink in China for around 2,000 years.

④ Construction first began on the Great Wall of China over 2,000 years ago to protect the people from raiding armies. It is actually a series of walls or fortifications running east to west that were eventually linked together. For some 5,500 miles it crosses deserts, grasslands, mountain regions, and more. The portions most recognizable today were from the Ming Dynasty that ended in 1644.

⑤ The Forbidden City served as the palace or royal home for 24 emperors of China. The walled city was known as "forbidden" because only the emperor could give you permission to enter or leave. The palace includes 980 buildings and covers over 7.8 million square feet. It is constructed of wood and marble, and over a million people were needed to build it.

In China, you see boats with what looks like sectioned, square sails. These are called *junks*, a type of boat design that has been used since 206 B.C. Though the word can refer to boats used for different purposes, from fishing to homes where people live, it is usually descriptive of the ships using the large sails with battens — strips of wood that reinforce and make it easier for the ship to sail into the wind.

Traditional clothing in China is often styled after a specific time period or dynasty. Dynasties were named for the ruling emperor. Here the hat with flower and tassels is from the Qing dynasty, which ruled from 1644 to 1912. Use of colors, materials like silk, even the patterns and style of the clothing have meaning. Dragons are often associated with royalty. The number of dragon claws often reflected the position of power of the person wearing it.

The most important holiday for the people of China is the Chinese New Year. It marks the end of winter and lasts for 15 days, with the last day being the celebration of the Lantern Festival! Beginning in either January or February, it is a very special time for families and friends. There is a 12-year cycle of names for each Chinese New Year, based on the following animals: rat, ox, tiger, rabbit, dragon, snake, horse, ram, monkey, rooster, dog, and pig.

Silk has been produced in China for over 4,000 years. Silkworm cocoons have been found in the tombs of royalty. Silk is produced by silkworms, which love to eat the leaves of the mulberry tree. They produce a silk thread that is woven into garments, and even some maps and royal decrees. Silk has been highly valued, and was kept secret from other countries for thousands of years as they sought this precious silk for kings and other royals. The secret finally was revealed and the skill of silk weaving spread to Japan, India, and finally into Europe.

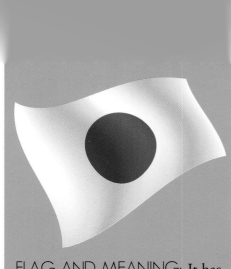

FLAG AND MEANING: It has a white background with a large red disk (representing the sun without rays) in the center. The Japanese characters that make up the name of the country mean "sun origin." This is why Japan is sometimes called the "Land of the Rising Sun."

Capital City	Tokyo
Government System	A parliamentary government with a constitutional monarchy
Primary Languages	Japanese
Population	127,368,088
Monetary Unit	Yen
Area	234,825 sq. miles
National Symbol	Red sun disc; chrysanthemum
National Anthem	"Kimigayo" ("The Emperor's Reign")
Largest City	Tokyo 8,949,447

Japan is an archipelago or chain of islands made up of four main islands (**Honshu**, **Hokkaido**, **Kyushu**, and **Shikoku**) and over 6,800 smaller ones. Mostly mountainous and rugged, Japan is impacted by volcanic activity, typhoons, and earthquakes. Some of these quakes can be severe, creating massive tsunamis. The worst in recent history happened in March 2011, and hit the northeast portion of Honshu Island, killing thousands of people and causing great damage to property. **Okinawa**, located very close to China, is actually a chain of hundreds of islands that belong to Japan.

① Starting in 1964, Japan has created a railway line to connect much of the country, even extending to the islands of Honshu and Kyushu. Called *Shinkansen* or the "Bullet Train," these trains can reach speeds of just over 180 mph. To make this rail transportation even faster and more efficient across the country, they are constantly expanding, and testing is being done that could have the trains traveling over 200 mph!

From the 17th to the 20th centuries, Japanese artists created beautiful woodcut print images and paintings known as *ukiyo-e*. The name means "floating world pictures" and refers to the temporary nature of beauty in the world. Woodcuts could be mass-produced affordably to be enjoyed by many.

This island country has been actively researching how to make buildings safer than the traditional wooden buildings for decades. Northeastern portions of the main island were devastated in 2011 by an earthquake and tsunami, collapsing buildings, killing thousands, and damaging a nuclear complex.

Christianity in Japan goes back as far as 1549. Francis Xavier was one of 20 Franciscan monks in Japan around that time. They established missions and a center in Nagasaki. When Christianity was outlawed, many Christians met secretly. The beliefs of Christ were kept by the *Kakure Kirishitan* or "hidden Christians."

For a time, Christianity was protected by the shogunate (the shogun warriors). However by 1597, persecutions against Christians became severe. The 26 martyrs of Japan were tortured and crucified because of their faith in Christ. A mark of the cross on the Himeji Castle is a sign that a Christian lived secretly there.

The first Protestant missionary in Japan was Dr. James Curtis Hepburn. He arrived in 1859 as a medical missionary, opening a special clinic near present-day Tokyo. He also helped create an English-Japanese dictionary, and later assisted with a Protestant Bible translation into Japanese.

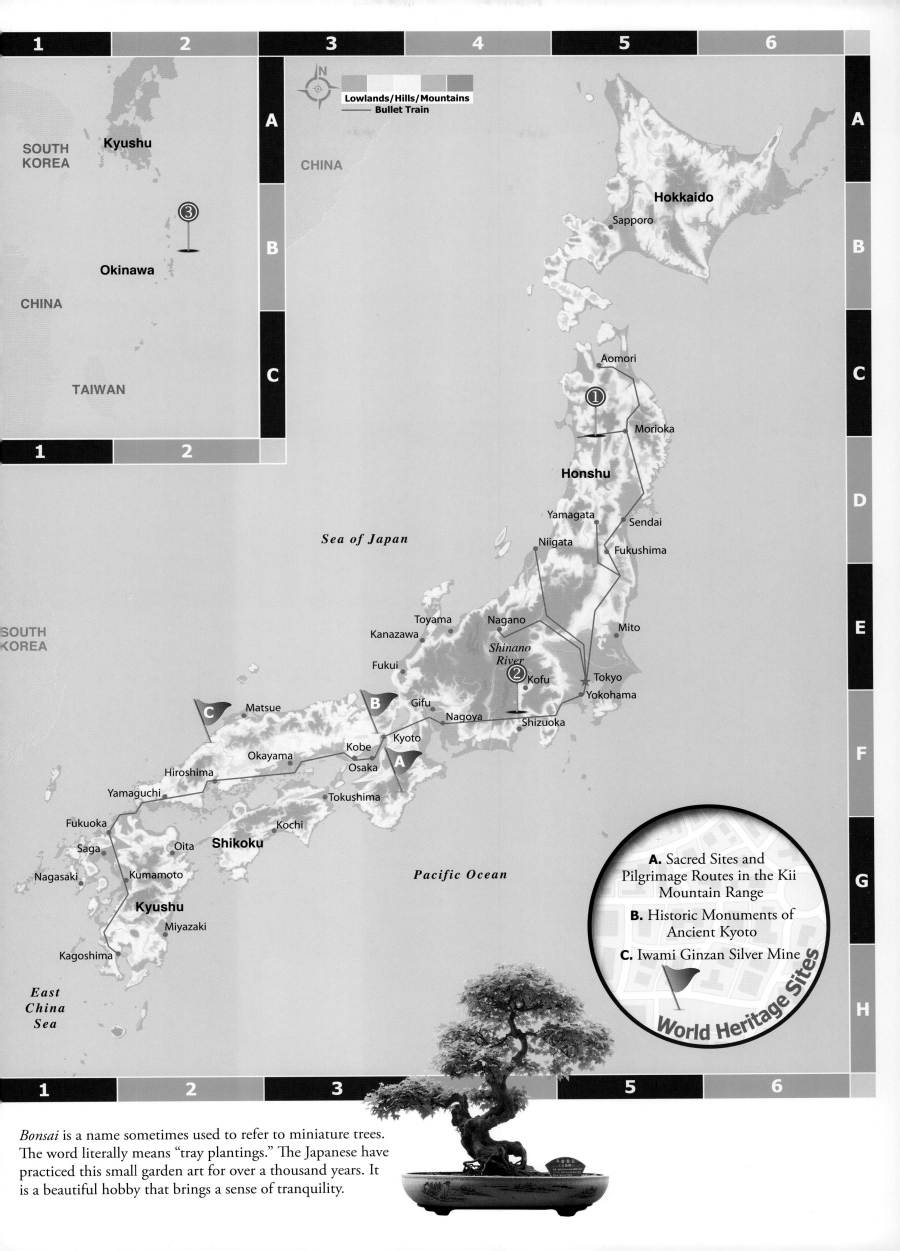

1 **2** **3** **4** **5** **6**

A

Lowlands/Hills/Mountains
— Bullet Train

SOUTH KOREA

CHINA

Kyushu

B

③

Okinawa

CHINA

C

TAIWAN

1 **2**

Hokkaido

Sapporo

Aomori

① Morioka

Honshu

Yamagata Sendai
Niigata Fukushima

Mito

Toyama Nagano
Kanazawa
Fukui *Shinano River* Tokyo
② Kofu Yokohama
Gifu Tokyo
B Nagoya
C Matsue Kyoto Shizuoka
Okayama Kobe
Hiroshima Osaka **A**
Yamaguchi Tokushima
Fukuoka Kochi
Saga Oita **Shikoku**
Nagasaki Kumamoto
Kyushu
Miyazaki
Kagoshima

East China Sea

Sea of Japan

Pacific Ocean

A. Sacred Sites and Pilgrimage Routes in the Kii Mountain Range
B. Historic Monuments of Ancient Kyoto
C. Iwami Ginzan Silver Mine

World Heritage Sites

Bonsai is a name sometimes used to refer to miniature trees. The word literally means "tray plantings." The Japanese have practiced this small garden art for over a thousand years. It is a beautiful hobby that brings a sense of tranquility.

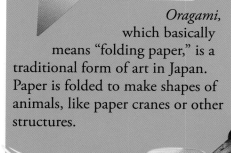

Japanese food was traditionally based on meatless dishes, usually with rice or noodles, and some side dishes. Seasonal availability of ingredients and the abundance of seafood influenced the Japanese diet. Sushi is a form of uncooked fish and other items paired with cooked and vinegared rice. The presentation of Japanese food was considered as important as the ingredients.

Oragami, which basically means "folding paper," is a traditional form of art in Japan. Paper is folded to make shapes of animals, like paper cranes or other structures.

The floor of a home in many Asian cultures has long been considered a central focus of the family. Though modern traditions have changed somewhat in Japanese culture, in traditional homes the tables are low to the ground with mats to sit upon. Because of this, the floors are kept very clean and one is required to take off his or her shoes, preventing dirt from being tracked into the home. Today you will find a mix of traditional homes and those with regular chairs, raised tables, and other styles of furniture from the West.

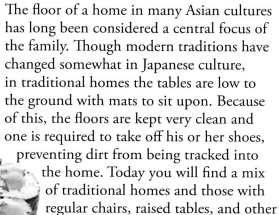

Sometimes called the Way of Tea, the Japanese tea ceremony is rooted deeply in the culture of the nation. It is not merely a time to drink tea, but involves all the preparation and attention to detail in the way it is served. In the ceremony, one serves *matcha* or a powdered green tea. The ritual is considered an art form.

Hina Matsuri is a Japanese festival on the 3rd of March when prayers are made for the health and happiness of young girls. It is a celebration of beautiful dolls that represent deeply held values of the people. A special ceremony of the dolls takes place when many of them are placed in small boats and placed in the sea.

Cranes are beautiful birds that nest in rivers and wetlands. This provides a means of protection as predators are unable to sneak up on them through the water. The red-crowned crane or Japanese crane is one of the rarest of these tall, slender birds. They migrate across the country, and in winter often are found in rice paddy fields.

② Mount Fuji is an active volcano on Honshu Island, and the highest mountain in Japan at 12,389 feet.

Mochi ➡

③ Dugongs are very similar to the manatees found in other parts of the world and are called sea cows, sea camels, or sea pigs. They are excellent parents, devoting much care to their calves. A female will give birth only every 3 to 7 years. This large marine mammal is found in warm coastal waters, grows to a length of almost 10 feet, and can live up to 70 years. Dugongs are found in 37 countries. Though protected in many places, populations are declining and have disappeared from some waters. They are struggling to survive in Okinawa.

Children's Day is celebrated here on May 5, where its name in Japanese is *Kodomo no hi*. It is a wondrous time when kites in the shape of colorful koi fish are flown along with vibrant banners.

Special foods are often shared on Children's Day including *chimaki* which are rice cakes wrapped in bamboo leaves, and *mochi*, pink rice cakes wrapped in oak leaves.

This goat-antelope is found in the thick forests of Honshu where they feed on acorns and leaves. They mark their territory in the woods with a substance that smells like vinegar. It drips out of glands near their eyes.

Japanese serow ➡

Manga is a form of comic book created in Japan. This is very popular throughout the country and around the world. It is a major industry and has its historical roots in early Japanese art. This type of illustrated book can focus on almost any subject, including history, science fiction, fantasy, detective mysteries, horror, and even business-related themes. Animations or cartoons that are presented in a motion format in Japan are called *anime*.

MALAYSIA

Comprised of 13 states and three territories, Malaysia is made up of **Peninsular Malaysia** and **Malaysian Borneo**. The South China Sea separates these two areas. Once under the authority of the British government in the 18th century, it became the independent Federation of Malaya in 1957. The name was changed to Malaysia in 1963, and it has been a vibrant, growing nation ever since. The country has a thriving science and medical industry, as well as tourism.

1 In the capital city, two huge buildings rise 1,483 feet into the skyline. Called the Petronas Towers, they are some of the tallest buildings in the world. Between the 41st and 42nd floors is a double-decker skybridge you can visit, the highest such bridge in the world.

2 The largest identified cave chamber in the world is the Sarawak Chamber in the Gunung Mulu National Park. The chamber is within the Gua Nasib Bagus (Good Luck Cave) on the island of Borneo. It's approximately 2,300 feet long, 1,300 feet wide, and some 230 feet high.

FLAG AND MEANING: There are 14 equal horizontal stripes of red and white; there is a blue rectangle in the upper left corner bearing a yellow crescent and a yellow, 14-pointed star. The 14 stripes stand for the equal status in the federation of the 13 member states and the federal government, and the 14 points on the star represent the unity between these entities. The crescent is a traditional symbol of Islam. Blue symbolizes the unity of the Malay people, and yellow is the royal color of Malay rulers.

Capital City	Kuala Lumpur
Government System	Constitutional monarchy
Primary Languages	Bahasa Malaysia, English, and Chinese
Population	29,179,952
Monetary Unit	Malaysian ringgit
Area	204,957 sq. miles
National Symbol	Tiger
National Anthem	"Negaraku" ("My Country"); the full version is only performed in the presence of the king.
Largest City	Kuala Lumpur 1,674,621

The Rafflesia is one of the largest flowers in the world, some reaching over three feet across. It is a well-known symbol of Malaysia, seen on stamps and coins. A rainforest flower, rather than giving a fragrant scent, the smell is described as foul or stinky at best!

Rempah is a spicy paste used in many Malaysian recipes. It is made by grinding or pounding garlic and shallots, and mixing in some other spices like cinnamon, coriander, cumin, ginger, lemon grass, peppercorns, turmeric, and more! Sometimes the mix is fried in oil or used to add flavor to meat or meals with curry.

The first Christians to reach Malaysia were here as early as the 7th century! Persian traders often included Nestorian Christians, and therefore many believe they may have had an influence here. The Nestorian Church was perhaps the world's largest church at the time, spanning from the Mediterranean all the way to China.

In 1511, the Portuguese sent people to this region to expand their influence in the world. They conquered the region of Melaka, which was central to those traveling to China and India. Included in those who came to inhabit the area were those sent to minister to the needs of the Roman Catholic population.

The Basel Mission Society began their ministry to the migrant Chinese residents here in 1882. During this time both Catholic and Protestant missions expanded throughout the region. This helped extend the influence of the gospel to a region of the world that has a fairly large Muslim population.

N

Lowlands / Hills / Mountains

CAMBODIA

A

THAILAND

South China Sea

B

Kota Baharu

Kota Kinabalu

Sandakan

George Town

C

Kuala Terengganu

Peninsula Malaysia

Malaysian Borneo

② Tawau

Ipoh

①

Kuantan

Kuala Lumpur ★

Pahang

Seremban

A

Rajang River

③

Kuching

INDONESIA

Melaka

Johor Bahru

SINGAPORE

A. Melaka and George Town, Historic Cities of the Straits of Malacca

B. Kinabalu Park

C. Archaeological Heritage of the Lenggong Valley

World Heritage Sites

The sun bear or honey bear is nocturnal, eating plants, ants, and honey at night and sleeping in the day. They are the smallest of the bear family. The yellow-orange fur on its chest inspired its name.

③ The Pasir Gudang World Kite Festival has been held on Bukit Layang-Layang (Kite Hill) in Bahasa Melayu since 1995. Malaysian gourds with sound slots are attached to the kites to create a whistling sound as the kites fly. In the past, kites were actually used for fishing. The Pasir Gudang Kite Museum opened seven years after the festival began.

Malaysia is the number one producer in the world of natural rubber. Synthetic rubber is made from petroleum, but natural rubber comes from the Hevea brasiliensis tree. The plantations here were established in 1877, with seeds being brought from the Amazon. These trees are "tapped" or cut, allowing the latex (natural rubber) to drip out. This is then harvested in buckets to be processed.

A Malay girl in a traditional *Baju Kurung* ➡

AUSTRALIA / OCEANIA

The region called Oceania or Australia/Oceania consists of the country of **Australia** and the surrounding area mostly within the Pacific Ocean, including **New Zealand**, **Papua New Guinea**, and literally thousands of islands. Islands are landforms surrounded by water. They can be created by breaking away from a larger landform or through volcanic activity on the ocean floor. Australia is the smallest, lowest, and flattest of the seven continents. Approximately 20 percent of the land is considered desert, while the other biomes or habitats include rainforests, cool temperature forests, coastal regions, and mountains, some of which are covered in snow.

① The Tasmanian devil is a fierce hunter and scavenger, about the size of a small dog. This carnivorous marsupial lives on the island of Tasmania, which is south of Melbourne, Australia, and the Bass Strait. Hunting at night, their screeches and screams can be quite terrifying.

② Mount Kosciuszko is the highest mountain on the continent of Australia at 7,310 feet (2,228 meters). The first successful ascent was in 1840. It is a fairly easy path to the top, and one is able to walk to the summit in a day, or even to ride a chairlift.

Except for polar regions, sea turtles are found around the world. All varieties are listed as endangered. Male sea turtles never return to shore after hatching, but females lay their eggs along coastal shorelines every two to four years. They have life spans of up to 80 years. They live mostly underwater, but must surface to breathe.

③ Made of limestone (calcium carbonate), reefs are formed when various algae, clams, corals, sponges, and other creatures cement themselves together in warm, shallow seas. The Great Barrier Reef is considered one of the seven natural wonders of the world, and is the world's largest coral reef. It is found off the eastern coast of Queensland, Australia, and is longer than the Great Wall of China. It is over 1,200 miles long, and is the only living organism that can be seen from space! Reefs thrive where there are warm, salty waters with lots of sunlight. Fish, whales, sea snakes, dolphins, sea turtles, and more make a home in or near the reef. Unfortunately, the health of the reef is being affected by pollution, too much fishing, and pressures from predatory species like the crown-of-thorns starfish that preys upon the growing coral. Any threat to the reef impacts an integrated group of sea creatures.

BIOME
Coral Reefs

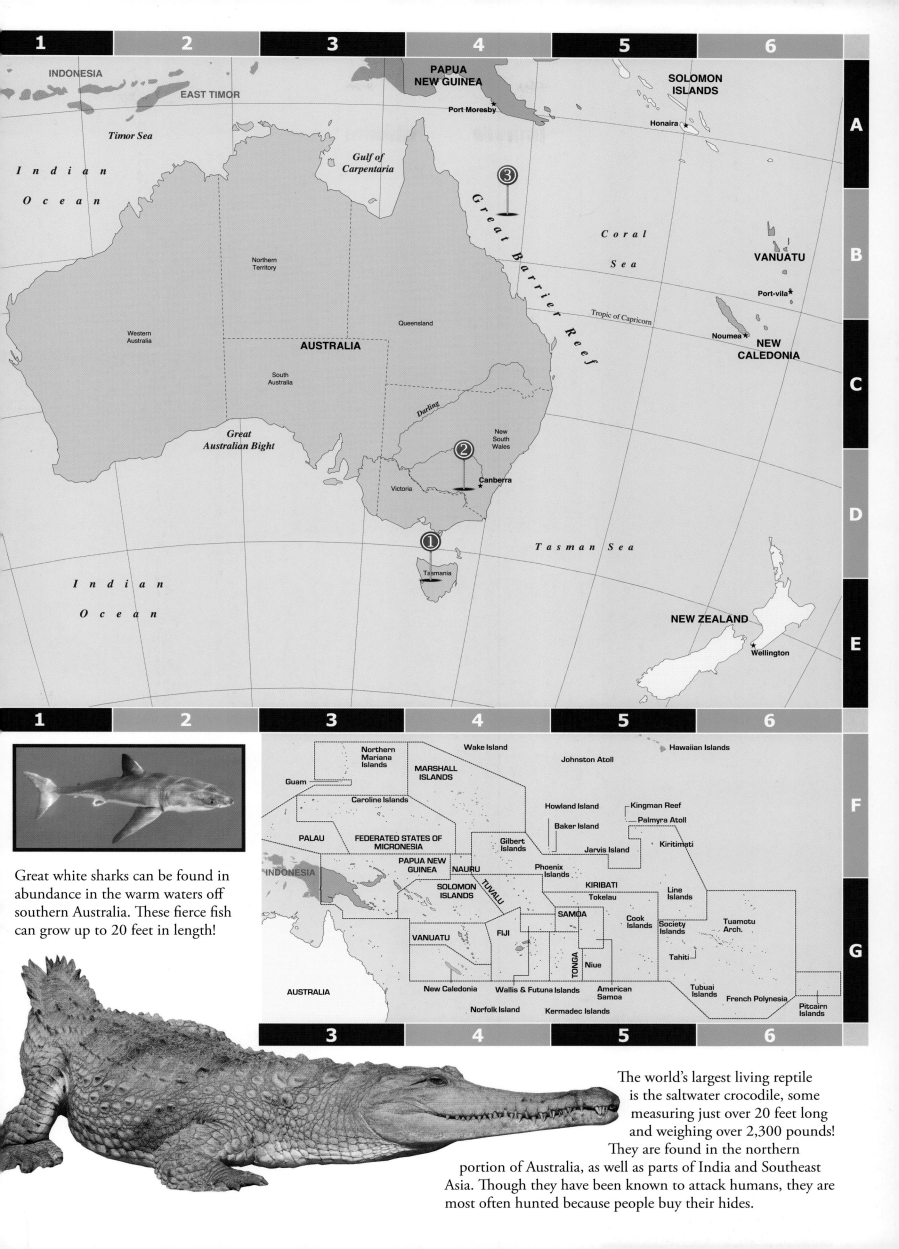

INDONESIA

EAST TIMOR

Timor Sea

Indian Ocean

PAPUA NEW GUINEA

Port Moresby ★

SOLOMON ISLANDS

Honaira ★

A

Gulf of Carpentaria

③

Great Barrier Reef

Coral Sea

VANUATU

B

Port-vila ★

Tropic of Capricorn

Northern Territory

Noumea ★

NEW CALEDONIA

C

Western Australia

Queensland

AUSTRALIA

South Australia

Great Australian Bight

Darling

New South Wales

②

Victoria

Canberra ★

D

①

Tasman Sea

Indian Ocean

Tasmania

NEW ZEALAND

Wellington ★

E

Great white sharks can be found in abundance in the warm waters off southern Australia. These fierce fish can grow up to 20 feet in length!

Wake Island

Hawaiian Islands

Northern Mariana Islands

MARSHALL ISLANDS

Johnston Atoll

Guam

Caroline Islands

Howland Island

Kingman Reef

Palmyra Atoll

F

PALAU

FEDERATED STATES OF MICRONESIA

Gilbert Islands

Baker Island

Jarvis Island

Kiritimati

INDONESIA

PAPUA NEW GUINEA

NAURU

Phoenix Islands

KIRIBATI

Line Islands

SOLOMON ISLANDS

TUVALU

Tokelau

Cook Islands

Society Islands

Tuamotu Arch.

VANUATU

FIJI

SAMOA

TONGA

Niue

American Samoa

Tahiti

Tubuai Islands

French Polynesia

Pitcairn Islands

G

AUSTRALIA

New Caledonia

Wallis & Futuna Islands

Norfolk Island

Kermadec Islands

The world's largest living reptile is the saltwater crocodile, some measuring just over 20 feet long and weighing over 2,300 pounds! They are found in the northern portion of Australia, as well as parts of India and Southeast Asia. Though they have been known to attack humans, they are most often hunted because people buy their hides.

It is blue with the flag of the United Kingdom in the upper left side quadrant and a large seven-pointed star in the lower hoist-side quadrant known as the Commonwealth or Federation Star, representing the federation of the colonies of Australia in 1901. The star depicts one point for each of the six original states and one representing all of Australia's internal and external territories. On the right half is a representation of the Southern Cross constellation in white.

Capital City	Canberra
Government System	Federal parliamentary democracy and a commonwealth realm
Primary Languages	English
Population	22,015,576
Monetary Unit	Australian Dollar
Area	4,810,171 sq. miles
National Symbol	Southern Cross constellation (five, seven-pointed stars); kangaroo; emu
National Anthem	"Advance Australia Fair"
Largest City	Sydney 4,605,992

82

The Commonwealth of Australia is a country that includes the primary continent of Australia, as well as the island of **Tasmania** and several smaller islands. These lands were first inhabited by the aboriginal or indigenous Australian peoples. Dutch explorers who happened upon the land in 1606, and by 1770 Great Britain began settling many people here, including over 160,000 prisoners in the years to come. Many other immigrants also came for various reasons, including a gold rush in the late 1800s. Australia is now a strong and thriving country. The name comes from the Latin word *australis*, which means "southern." Because Australia lies south of the equator, many people call it "the land down under."

① Opened in 1973 and built on Sydney Harbor with a design inspired by great sailing ships, the Sydney Opera House stands as one of the most distinctive buildings of the 20th century. Multifunctional and drawing visitors from around the world, it is a UNESCO World Heritage Site.

② The River Murray is the longest river in Australia. It is approximately 1,800 miles in length.

Bushfood is a term used to describe food native to Australia. It is also called bush tucker, and includes fruits such as kutjera and quandong, and meats like crocodile and kangaroo!

← Quandong

Most marsupials live in Australia, including the Leadbeater's Possum, koalas, wallabies, and wombats. These are mammals that most often have a pouch to carry their young.

There are certain bats in Australia that don't use echolocation to find food. They have larger eyes to find it, even when feeding at night. These megabats are also known as fruit bats or flying foxes. The grey-headed flying fox is the largest bat found in Australia and loves to suck the juice from fruit.

Fruit bat ➡

Wallaby ➡

Captain James Cook was an English explorer and cartographer (mapmaker) in the 1700s. He stood out among many sailors of the time, not allowing bad words on his ships. His wife gave him a prayer book when he sailed. From this he named many of the places on the coast of Australia, including Trinity Bay, Pentecost Islands, and Whitsunday Passage.

John Clifford Peel was a pilot in the early days of aviation. In 1917, he suggested that airplanes be used to bring care to people in the Outback. The Australian Inland Mission began a Flying Doctor Service in 1928 based on this suggestion. This ministry still helps areas hard to reach because of the rocky terrain.

Elizabeth Ward helped minister to women in Australia around the turn of the 20th century. A part of her assistance was providing midnight meals to those in need. She eventually helped the elderly find the benefits they needed to survive. She often wrote about how the poor were in want of both material and spiritual provision.

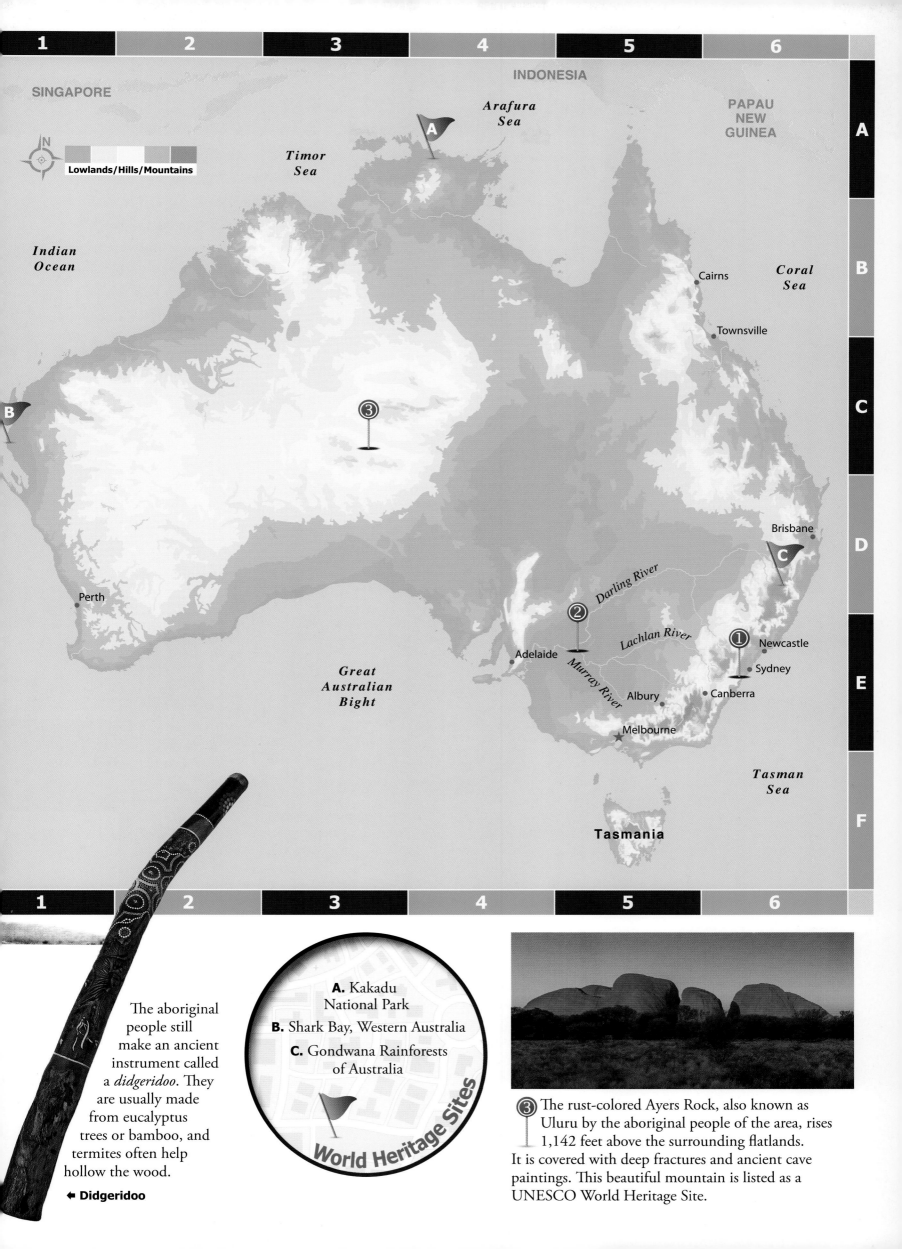

INDONESIA

SINGAPORE

Arafura Sea

Timor Sea

A

Indian Ocean

N

Lowlands/Hills/Mountains

PAPAU NEW GUINEA

Cairns

Coral Sea

Townsville

B

③

Brisbane

C

Darling River

Lachlan River

②

Adelaide

Murray River

Perth

Great Australian Bight

Albury

① Newcastle

Sydney

Canberra

Melbourne

Tasman Sea

Tasmania

A
B
C
D
E
F

The aboriginal people still make an ancient instrument called a *didgeridoo*. They are usually made from eucalyptus trees or bamboo, and termites often help hollow the wood.

← **Didgeridoo**

A. Kakadu National Park

B. Shark Bay, Western Australia

C. Gondwana Rainforests of Australia

World Heritage Sites

③ The rust-colored Ayers Rock, also known as Uluru by the aboriginal people of the area, rises 1,142 feet above the surrounding flatlands. It is covered with deep fractures and ancient cave paintings. This beautiful mountain is listed as a UNESCO World Heritage Site.

FLAG AND MEANING: It is blue with the flag of the U.K. in the upper left side quadrant with four red, five-pointed stars edged in white centered in the outer half of the flag. The stars represent the Southern Cross constellation.

Capital City	Wellington
Government System	Parliamentary democracy and a commonwealth realm
Primary Languages	English
Population	4,327,944
Monetary Unit	New Zealand dollar
Area	166,347 sq. miles
National Symbol	Southern Cross constellation (four five-pointed stars); kiwi (bird)
National Anthem	New Zealand has two national anthems with equal status; "God Defend New Zealand" and "God Save the Queen".
Largest City	Auckland 1,397,300

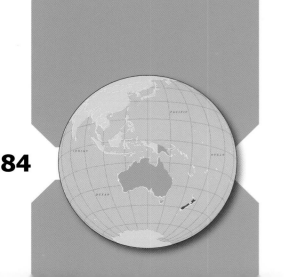

New Zealand is made up of two islands, the **North Island** with the city of Wellington, the capital, and the major port city of **Auckland**; and the larger, less-populated **South Island**, with the magnificent **Southern Alps** rising over the grasslands. **Wellington** is the most southern national capital in the world. There are approximately ten times as many sheep as people in this wondrous country. The landscapes vary wildly, with miles of coastline, subtropical forests, open plains, rolling hills, large mountain ranges, and glaciers. Fjords are also found in New Zealand. These are narrow bodies of water found around the world, often coming from the ocean or large inland sea. Fjords were carved by glaciers which then filled with water.

Geothermal power is generated from deep within the earth. It often surfaces in areas that have hot springs, geysers, and other places where steam is released from the earth's crust. In New Zealand there are several areas that produce such natural power that can be used for generating electricity. In **Rotorua**, there are geysers, hot springs, and mud pools. These were used long ago by the Māori people who were able to use the natural heat for bathing and cooking.

← **Kiwi bird**

About the size of a chicken, the flightless kiwi bird is a national symbol of New Zealand. They are currently endangered because their forest habitats were cut back in the past, but are being protected in special reserves and national parks.

Māori are the indigenous or native people of New Zealand. Their culture is tribal and the tribes are known as iwi. Many visitors to the country are able to see how the Māori cook food on hot stones, and watch their unique singing and dancing. Their culture has been rooted here for many hundreds of years.

John Ronald Reuel Tolkien was a writer and professor in England. He wrote *The Lord of the Rings* trilogy. Partly because of his influence, C.S. Lewis, author of *The Chronicles of Narnia* series and a former atheist, came to Christ. J.R.R. Tolkien's books have been transformed into movies, filmed in New Zealand using the unique and wondrous landscapes here.

In the early 1800s, Christian missionaries came to try and reach the Māori people with the Gospel. By 1814, the Church Mission Society developed a presence here, led by Samuel Marsden. This was done with the approval and protection of Ruatara, chief of the Ngāpuhi people.

Kiwifruit is a fruit about the size of a large chicken egg. It originally came from China, where New Zealander Mary Isabel Fraser had been visiting a mission school in Yichang. She was principal of the Wanganui Girls' College, and brought the seeds back with her. They were first planted here in 1906 and now are very much associated with the country.

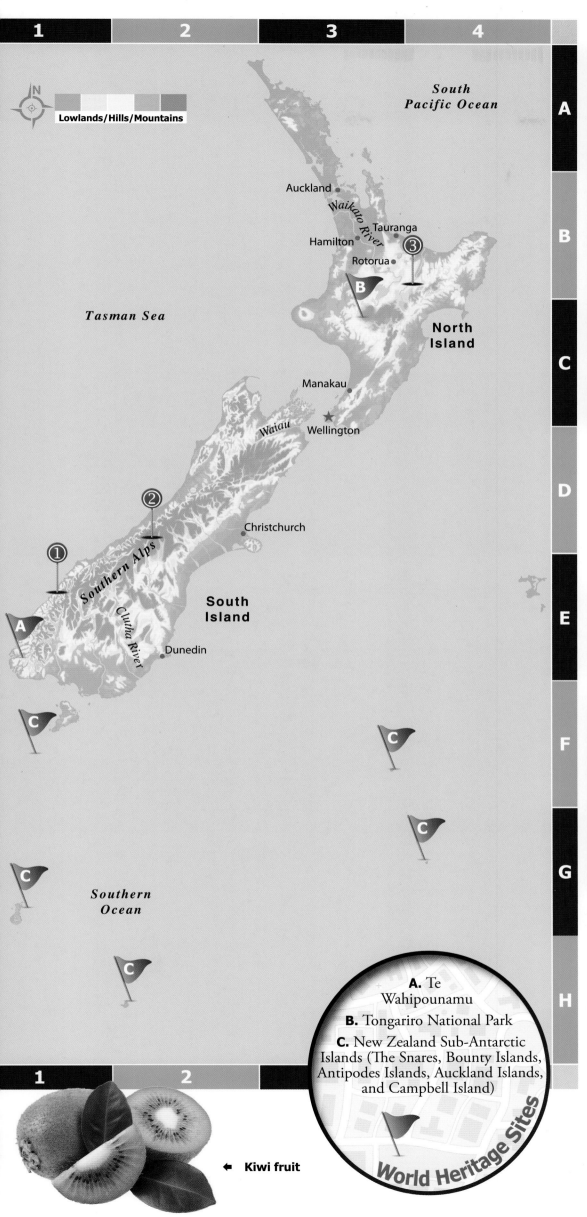

1 | **2** | **3** | **4**

Lowlands/Hills/Mountains

South Pacific Ocean

Auckland

Waikato River

Tauranga

Hamilton

Rotorua

B

Tasman Sea

North Island

Manakau

Waiau

Wellington

D

Christchurch

Southern Alps

A

Clutha River

South Island

Dunedin

C

C

C

Southern Ocean

C

C

A. Te Wahipounamu

B. Tongariro National Park

C. New Zealand Sub-Antarctic Islands (The Snares, Bounty Islands, Antipodes Islands, Auckland Islands, and Campbell Island)

World Heritage Sites

1 | **2**

← **Kiwi fruit**

1 On the southwest coast of South Island, there is a fjord called Milford Sound. Its steep cliffs and beautiful waterfalls rise above the dark waters. The writer Rudyard Kipling called it the eighth wonder of the world.

2 Mount Cook is the tallest mountain in New Zealand, with its highest point at 12,316 feet. It is located in the Mount Cook (Aoraki) National Park, which is a part of the Southern Alps range. Sir Edmund Hillary used the mountains here to prepare for his historic Mount Everest climb. In 1953, he was the first to summit Everest along with Tenzing Norgay, a Sherpa guide.

3 *Waiotapu* is a geothermal region on the North Island. The name means "sacred waters" in the Māori language.

ANTARCTICA

Emperor penguins are the largest of the flightless birds, and can grow to nearly four feet.

In 1820, the first sightings of Antarctica occurred. The first actual landing happened about a year later when American captain John Davis stepped onto the ice. He was working as a seal hunter. The first team to reach the South Pole was led by Norwegian Roald Amundsen in 1911. This courageous explorer also was the first to cross the Northwest Passage, which he did between 1903 and 1906. He disappeared without a trace in 1928 while searching for survivors of a crash. The largest of Antarctica's subglacial lakes is called **Lake Vostok**, named after the Russian science station there. The freshwater lake is over 1,300 feet beneath the ice. The magnetic south pole is located near **Adelie Land** in Antarctica, moving about three miles each year.

Up to 90 percent of the earth's ice is found in the Antarctic ice cap, as is much of the earth's fresh water.

The wingless midge, an insect that is only about half an inch long, is called the largest land animal here since there are no land mammals!

① Mount Vinson is the highest mountain on the continent of Antarctica at 16,050 feet (4,892 meters). The first successful ascent was in 1966. Depending on the weather, it can take anywhere from two to four weeks to summit.

② The coldest temperature ever recorded on earth was here in July of 1983. The Russian research station Vostok noted that the temperature was a chilly -128.6 degrees F. It's so cold here in places that it is known as the world's driest desert. Water vapor in the air actually freezes!

The Antarctic krill are tiny creatures that thrive here in the cold waters. They are shrimplike, and though small, penguins, seals, squid, and whales need them to survive. Just one blue whale can eat several million a day!

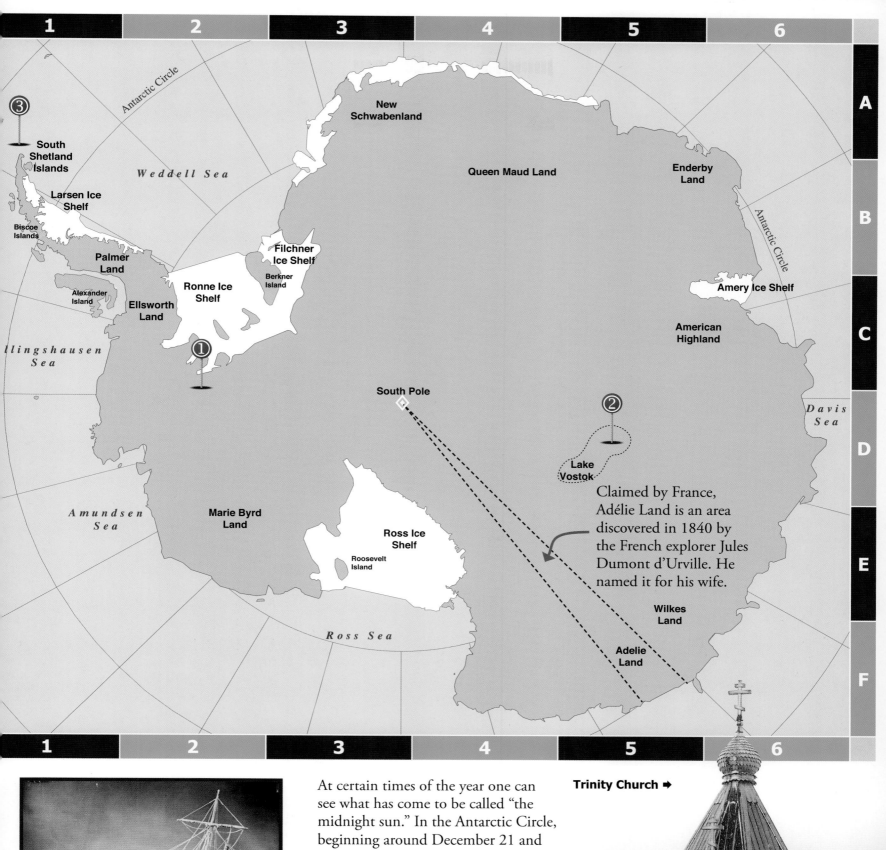

New Schwabenland

Queen Maud Land

Enderby Land

③
South Shetland Islands

Antarctic Circle

Weddell Sea

Larsen Ice Shelf

Biscoe Islands

Palmer Land

Filchner Ice Shelf

Berkner Island

Amery Ice Shelf

Antarctic Circle

Alexander Island

Ronne Ice Shelf

Ellsworth Land

American Highland

Illingshausen Sea

①

Davis Sea

South Pole ◇

②
Lake Vostok

Amundsen Sea

Marie Byrd Land

Ross Ice Shelf

Roosevelt Island

Claimed by France, Adélie Land is an area discovered in 1840 by the French explorer Jules Dumont d'Urville. He named it for his wife.

Wilkes Land

Adelie Land

Ross Sea

A

B

C

D

E

F

The Norwegian Lutheran Church on Grytviken, located on South Georgia and the South Sandwich Islands, first opened on Christmas Day 1913. The church conducted the funeral service for Sir Ernest Shackleton, who had led the famous British expedition of 1914–1916 to Antarctica. His ship, *Endurance*, was caught in the ice and crushed, though not a single life was lost.

At certain times of the year one can see what has come to be called "the midnight sun." In the Antarctic Circle, beginning around December 21 and lasting several months, the sun is still visible even at midnight. This depends on whether or not there is clear weather. The midnight sun can also be seen on the other side of the world in the Arctic Circle from around June 21 and lasting several months.

③ Out of a need for a permanent church on Antarctica, plans for Trinity Church began in the 1990s. Following its construction, it was taken apart and shipped to its location on the largest of the South Shetland Islands for reconstruction. This small Russian Orthodox church holds about 30 worshipers and officially opened on King George Island in 2004.

Trinity Church ➡

BIOMES OF THE WORLD

Biomes (short for biological homes) are habitats or unique homes where certain plants and animals live. God has designed this wonderful diversity into His creation. Different patterns across biomes can be seen depending on where you live in relation to east and west, or north and south. If an ocean is just west of you, often it will produce much rainfall to water the forests. If this is near a large mountain range, one side may be lush forest and the other side may actually be very dry. The dry side of a mountain is called the "rain shadow." You might notice too that the farther north one goes from the equator, the lower the average temperature range is and seasonal changes are much greater. The map on these two pages shows where these special homes can be found. What's in your neighborhood?

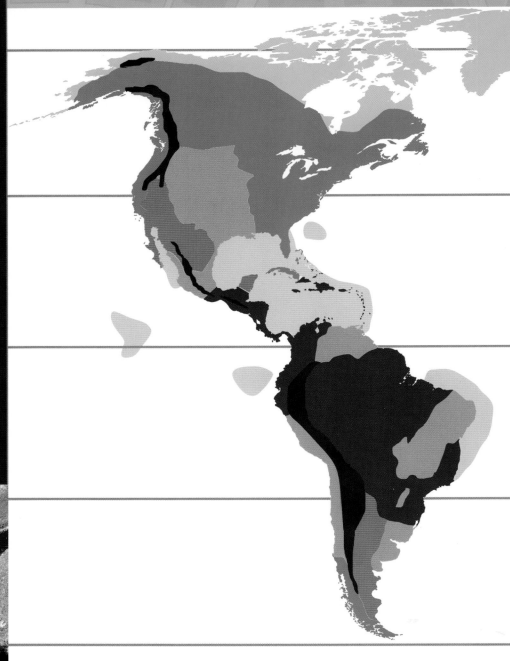

Rivers & Lakes

Grasslands

Desert

BIOME Rain Forest

These brooks, creeks, and streams are fed by rainfall and snowfall, taking this water over hundreds and thousands of miles to lakes and oceans. The plants and creatures that thrive in these waterways affect the land that surrounds them. The Nile River in Egypt has provided rich life in the desert to the communities alongside it for thousands of years.

Whether called pampas, prairies, steppes, or savannas, they are found where there is too little rain for trees and more rain than a desert receives. Enough rain falls to support grass but not trees. These are some of the richest soils in the world. Large farmlands often inhabit former grasslands because there is enough rain to nourish crops but not enough to wash away nutrients in the soil.

They might be hot or cold, but these are always places that receive less than 10 inches of rain or snow a year. There are plants, but these are widely spaced and usually need little water. Some were designed by God to release seed just as the sparse rain falls, and to grow quickly. Even animals are designed to thrive here, with the spadefoot toad growing from egg to adult in under 10 days!

The forests here have lots of rain and trees that never lose their leaves. The soil quality in rainforests is actually very poor. There is so much rain that the minerals needed for plants to grow is often washed away. This is called "leaching." Because of this, many plants were designed to grow in the branches of other plants!

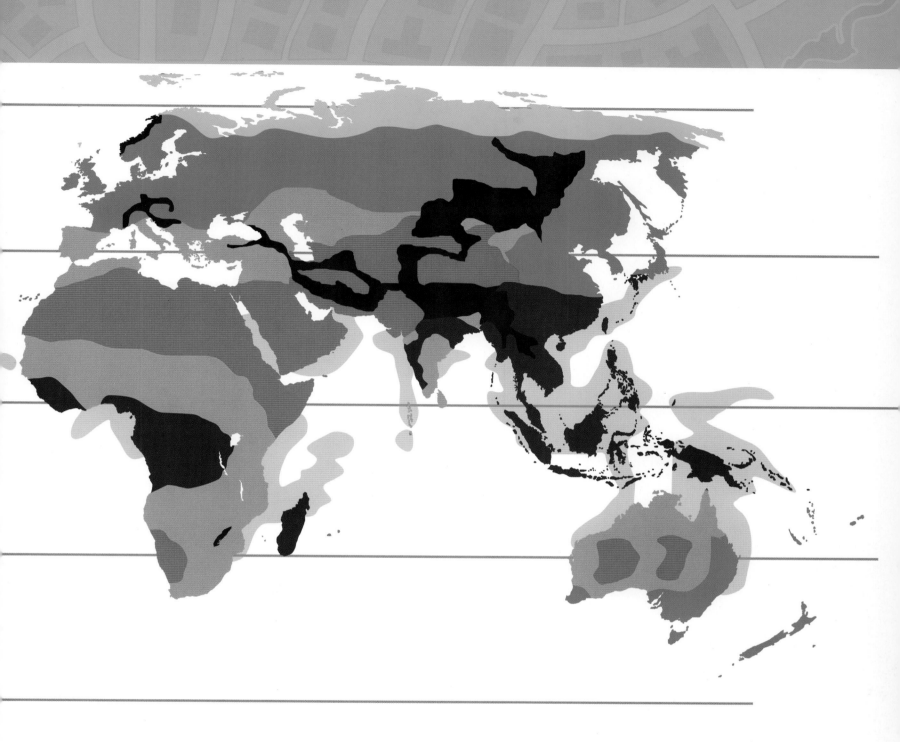

Forest

These include the coniferous forests that have trees with cones and needles. The trees and plants here were designed by God to survive often harsh, cold winters. It also includes the deciduous forests that have trees that lose their leaves in fall. The oak, maple, and walnut trees included have been used to build homes and other structures for centuries.

Coral Reefs

Life thrives in these reefs, which are formed when various algae, clams, corals, sponges, and other creatures cement themselves together in warm, shallow seas. Fringing reefs are those that are actually attached to the shore. Barrier reefs are found farther offshore. These are the biggest reefs in the ocean, and include Australia's Great Barrier Reef.

Mountains

Mountains are raised up areas of land formed either by volcanoes or the movement on the earth's crust. They can hold several biomes, such as Mount Kilimanjaro in Africa. The base is surrounded by rain forest. Above that is a deciduous forest. Farther still there is a coniferous forest at a higher elevation. Finally, the top of the mountain is covered in alpine tundra.

Arctic Tundra

These are lands with very cold climates and very few plants. However, the warmer months on the tundra actually are filled with wondrous life. The days of nearly 24 hours of sunlight in summer melt off the top frozen layer of ice. Then the permafrost thaws and becomes marshy places where large flocks of migrating birds come to nest.

GLOSSARY

↑ **Archipelago of Ang Thong, National Marine Park, Koh Samui, Thailand**

↑ **Sandstone butte in Monument Valley, Arizona, United States**

↑ **Aerial view of icebergs and glaciers at Cape York, Greenland**

↑ **Barrenjoey Isthmus that divides Pittwater from the Pacific, New South Wales, Australia**

archipelago: A group of islands close together in an ocean or sea.

bay: An area of water in a lake or sea that is partially encircled by land.

butte: A rocky mountain like a mesa but with a smaller, flat surface.

canyon: A gorge or valley with rocky, sloped sides.

cave: A tunnel or hollowed-out area underground, some with miles of connected caverns.

coastline (shoreline): The land at the edge of or surrounding a bay or ocean.

continent: There are seven continents on earth, which are large areas of land with various countries.

deserts: Deserts can be hot or cold, but they are most often dry places that receive less than 10 inches of rain each year.

fjord: Narrow waterways connected to the sea with tall, steep cliffs.

forests: Coniferous forests (forests with trees that have cones and needles), rainforests (forests with lots of rain and trees that never lose their leaves), and deciduous forests (forests with trees that lose their leaves in fall).

geyser: A hole in the ground that releases hot water and steam into the air from underground.

glacier: A river of ice that stays frozen all year and moves very slowly down mountain slopes.

grasslands: Grasslands cover about one-fourth of earth's land. They are found where there is too little rain for trees and more rain than a desert receives. In South America they are known as pampas. If you're in the United States, they are called prairies. In Russia they are called steppes. And in Africa they are called savannas.

gulf: An area of the sea or ocean that is partially surrounded by land but much larger than a bay.

hill: A mound of land raised above the surrounding landscape, and smaller than a mountain.

iceberg: A large portion of floating ice; often 90 percent of it is under water.

island: Islands are land forms surrounded by water. They can be created by breaking away from a larger landform or through volcanic activity on the ocean floor.

isthmus: A thin area of land with water on two sides and connecting two larger portions of land.

jungle: A thick forested area, often in tropical zones where it is always warm.

key: Small islands made from sand and coral structures.

knob: Like a hill, but smaller in size.

lake: A large body of fresh water enclosed by land.

marsh: A low-lying wetland filled with diverse life and covered in tall grasses.

mesa: A rocky mountain like a butte but with a larger, flat top.

mountains: Mountains are raised-up areas of land formed either by volcanic activity or movement on the earth's crust. The higher elevations of a mountain have less oxygen and less rainfall. This makes it more difficult for plants to grow at higher elevations.

oceans: Though the waters all cycle together, there are five distinct oceans recognized in the world, listed here in order of size: Pacific Ocean, Atlantic Ocean, Indian Ocean, Southern Ocean, and Arctic Ocean. These are filled with salty water that is not drinkable, and much diverse life is designed to thrive here.

peninsula: A large section of land that sticks far out into a large body of water.

plain: A broad flatland covered mostly with grasses rather than trees.

plateau: A large, flat area of land that is raised above the surrounding area.

reef (coral): Made of limestone (calcium carbonate), reefs are formed when various algae, clams, corals, sponges, and other creatures cement themselves together in warm, shallow seas.

rivers (brooks, creeks, streams): These water sources are fed by rainfall and snowfall, transporting large amounts of water over hundreds and thousands of miles. Smaller brooks and creeks merge to form streams, which merge to form rivers. These bring water on a continual basis to lakes and eventually to the ocean, moving down sloped mountains and hills. Along the way, many towns and cities have often been built that use the water to drink, for crops and animals, for fishing, and for transportation by boat.

sea: A large inland area of salt water, too small to be considered an ocean.

tundra: Cold climate lands with very few plants.

valley: The lower areas between hills and mountains.

volcano: A break in the ground that releases hot gas, ash, and lava from deep in the earth.

waterfall: A stream or river that flows over a cliff, either as one drop (a cataract) or in sloped steps down a hill or mountain (a cascade).

⬆ **Eruption of Castle Geyser in Yellowstone National Park, United States**

⬆ **Volcanic eruption, Anak Krakatau, Indonesia**

⬆ **Sharp mountain peaks and deep fjords on Lofoten Islands in Norway**

⬆ **Fish River Canyon, Namibia, Africa**

⬅ **The Great Rift Valley in Kenya, Africa**

*The following definitions reflect only the governmental systems of the countries found within this book.

commonwealth: A nation, state, or other political entity founded on law and united by a compact of the people for the common good.

communism: A system of government in which the state plans and controls the economy and a single — often authoritarian — party holds power. State controls are imposed with the elimination of private ownership of property or capital while claiming to make progress toward a higher social order in which all goods are equally shared by the people (i.e., a classless society).

constitutional: A government by or operating under an authoritative document (constitution) that sets forth the system of fundamental laws and principles that determines the nature, functions, and limits of that government.

constitutional democracy: A form of government in which the sovereign power of the people is spelled out in a governing constitution.

constitutional monarchy: A system of government in which a monarch is guided by a constitution whereby his/her rights, duties, and responsibilities are spelled out in written law or by custom.

democracy: A form of government in which the supreme power is retained by the people, but which is usually exercised indirectly through a system of representation and delegated authority periodically renewed.

federal (federation): A form of government in which sovereign power is formally divided — usually by means of a constitution — between a central authority and a number of constituent regions (states, colonies, or provinces) so that each region retains some management of its internal affairs. Differs from a confederacy in that the central government exerts influence directly upon both individuals as well as upon the regional units.

federal republic: A state in which the powers of the central government are restricted and in which the component parts (states, colonies, or provinces) retain a degree of self-government; ultimate sovereign power rests with the voters who chose their governmental representatives.

monarchy: A government in which the supreme power is lodged in the hands of a monarch who reigns over a state or territory, usually for life and by hereditary right. The monarch may be either a sole absolute ruler or a sovereign — such as a king, queen, or prince — with constitutionally limited authority.

parliamentary democracy: A political system in which the legislature (parliament) selects the government — a prime minister, premier, or chancellor along with the cabinet ministers — according to party strength as expressed in elections. By this system, the government acquires a dual responsibility: to the people as well as to the parliament.

parliamentary government (cabinet-parliamentary government): A government in which members of an executive branch (the cabinet and its leader — a prime minister, premier, or chancellor) are nominated to their positions by a legislature or parliament, and are directly responsible to it. This type of government can be dissolved at will by the parliament (legislature) by means of a no confidence vote, or the leader of the cabinet may dissolve the parliament if it can no longer function.

republic: A representative democracy in which the people's elected deputies (representatives), not the people themselves, vote on legislation.

*www.cia.gov - The World Factbook

Ukrainian girls wearing vyshyvankas at the Independence Day celebration

National Day Celebrations in Haugesund, Norway

Singapore National Day celebrations

Independence Day celebration in Itanagar, Arunachal Pradesh, India

Holidays (originally from "holy days") are days of celebration or honor or remembrance, for families, people groups, or nations. Here is a calendar of only a few of these most special days from around the world, celebrating cultures and nations.

January
1 – New Year's Day
6 – Epiphany
15 – Martin Luther King Jr. Day (U.S)
26 – Republic Day
26 – Australia Day
Chinese New Year (January – February)

February
2 – Candlemas
3 – Setsbun (Japan)
6 – Waitangi Day (New Zealand)
11 – National Foundation Day (Japan)
14 – Valentine's Day

March
1 – St. David's Day (Wales)
3 – Hina Matsuri (Japan)
6 – National Day (Ghana)
17 – St. Patrick's Day (Ireland)
23 – National Day (Pakistan)
25 – National Day (Greece)

April
4, 5 – Ch-ing Ming Festival (China)
23 – Egemenlik Bayrami (Turkey)
23 – St. George's Day (England)

May
1 – May Day (Europe)
3 – National Day (Poland)
5 – Kodomono-hi (Japan)
17 – National Day (Norway)

June
2 – Republic Day (Italy)
6 – National Day (Sweden)
23 – Midsummer's Eve

July
1 – National Day (Canada)
4 – U.S. Independence Day
9 – National Day (Argentina)
14 – Bastille Day (France)
21 – National Day (Belgium)

August
1 – National Day (Switzerland)
6 – National Day (Bolivia)
17 – National Day (Indonesia)
Raksha Bandhan (India) and Eisteddfod Day (Wales) are moving holidays.

September
7 – National Day (Brazil)
16 – National Day (Mexico)
18 – National Day (Chile)
30 – National Day (Botswana)
Rosh Hashanah (Jewish) is a holiday that changes based on the moon's cycle.

October
1 – National Day (China)
9 – National Day (Uganda)
12 – National Day (Spain)
12 – Columbus Day
24 – United Nations Day
24 – National Day (Zambia)
26 – National Day (Austria)
31 – Halloween (All Hallows Eve)
Thanksgiving (Canada) is the second Monday in October.

November
1 – All Saints' Day
2 – All Souls' Day
5 – Guy Fawkes Day (United Kingdom)
30 – St. Andrew's Day (Scotland)
Thanksgiving (U.S.) is the fourth Thursday in November.

December
6 – National Day (Finland)
6 – St. Nicholas' Day
9 – National Day (Tanzania)
12 – National Day (Kenya)
13 – St. Lucia's Day
24 – Christmas Eve
25 – Christmas Day
26 – St. Stephen's Day
26 – Boxing Day
31 – New Year's Eve
Hanukkah (Jewish) and Kwanzaa (African American) are moving holidays.

St David's Day Celebration ➡

INDEX

Within this index you will find page numbers for each entry. Those places found on the maps include a grid reference. Note the following example:

Turkmenistan **59-D2**

You will find Turkmenistan on page 59. Then trace your fingers from the letter D and the number 2 on the grid surrounding the map to find its general location.

Photo Credits: T-top, B-bottom, L-left, R-right, C-center

All images Shutterstock.com unless stated.
All country maps by AridOcean.com
istock.com: pg. 3 C, pg. 10 RB, pg. 40 CB, pg. 57 BR, pg. 63 BR, pg. 68 BL, pg. 72 TR, pg. 74 CR
NASA: pg. 11CR, pg. 29 BL
NOAA; pg. 86 TL
Superstock.com: pg. 10 L, pg. 66 CL
Wikimedia Commons: pg. 6 CR (2), pg. 10 CT, pg. 12 C, pg. 18 CR, pg. 19 LB (2), pg. 19 CB, pg. 20 L, pg. 20 B, pg. 22 BR, pg. 26 TR, pg. 26 M (2), pg. 30 TR, pg. 32 C, pg. 34 C, pg. 36 TL, pg. 36 BL, pg. 36 C, pg. 37 TL, pg. 40 CR, pg. 42 C, pg. 44 BL, pg 44 BR, pg. 45 C (bug), pg. 48 C, pg. 49 CB, pg. 51 BL, pg. 52 TR, pg. 53 BR, pg. 55 BR, pg. 56 CR, pg. 62 M (panorama), pg. 62 CL, pg. 62 BL, pg. 63 TR, pg. 64 CB, pg. 65 CB, pg. 65 CR, pg. 68 TL, pg. 68 TL, pg. 71 B, pg. 74 T, pg. 74 CL, pg. 76, TR, pg. 76 CR, pg. 77 CL, pg. 79 CL, pg. 80 TR, pg. 82 T, pg. 82 CB, pg. 86 TR, pg. 86 CR, pg. 86 B, pg. 87 BL, pg. 90 L (icebergs), pg. 91 T, pg. 93 all
Images from Wikimedia Commons are used under the CC-BY-SA-3.0 license or the GNU Free Documentation License, Version 1.3.

All country data from introductory green sidebars is from the Central Intelligence Agency (cia.gov).

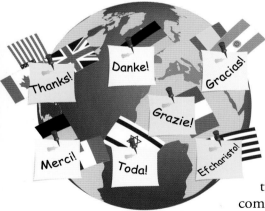

It is with our deepest appreciation that we thank Marie and David Hazell of My Father's World for their inspiration, commitment, and partnership with us in creating this unique children's atlas. Their vision and awareness of a need for a product like this in the Christian education community was essential in the creative process. Their skillful insights and suggestions on text, colors, maps, highlighted countries, and age-appropriate presentations helped to not only shape the design and content of this atlas, but also improved its effectiveness as an educational resource. We hope you have enjoyed this book and that it has been a blessing to your family!

MY FATHER'S WORLD®
www.mfwbooks.com

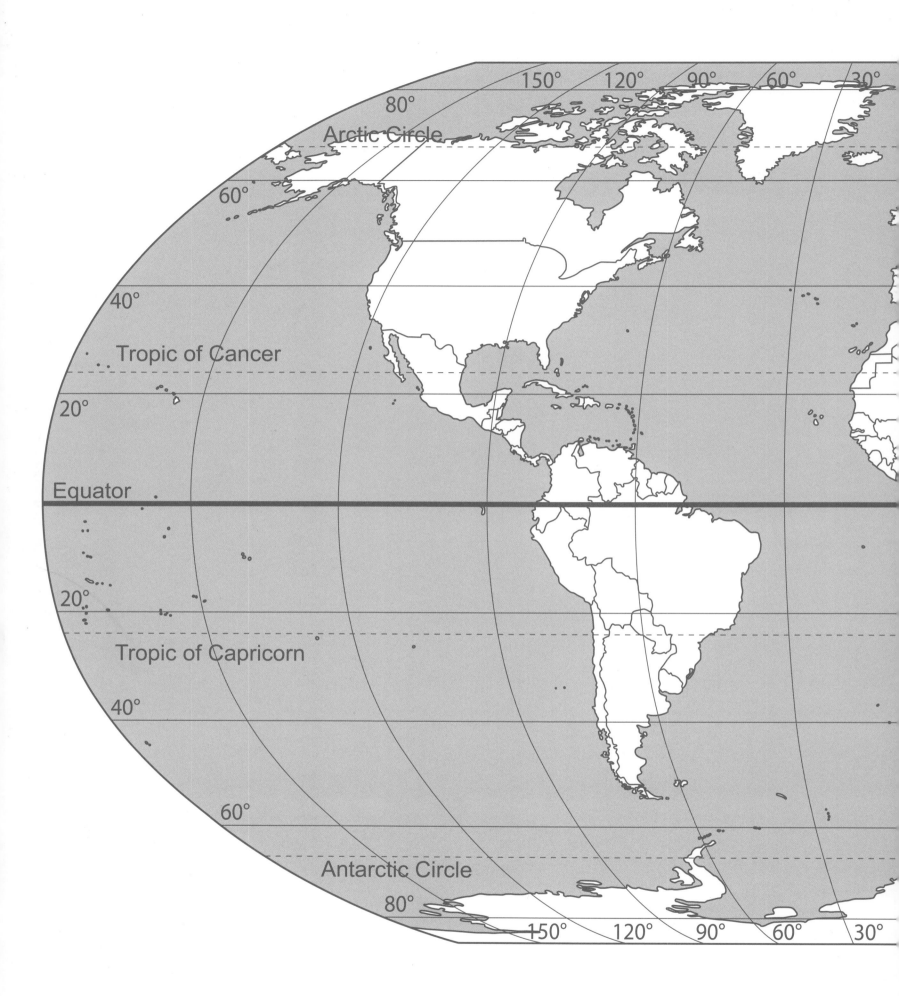

150°   120°   90°   60°   30°

80°

Arctic Circle

60°

40°

Tropic of Cancer

20°

Equator

20°

Tropic of Capricorn

40°

60°

Antarctic Circle

80°

150°   120°   90°   60°   30°